'Absolutely terrific book. Little masterpiece. In this enchanting book, William Bloom shares historic and personal details about the mythic existence and contemporary reality of our invisible spiritual friends with whom we share this planet. I highly recommend this book for several reasons, but most of all because I am grateful that someone finally took up the task of separating new age nonsense from spiritual reality.'

Caroline Myss PhD, author of *Anatomy of the Spirit* and *Why People Don't Heal and How They Can*

'With each new book, William Bloom continues to enhance his position as one of the finest modern writers on spiritual themes. This book can only further his reputation. *Working with Angels* is outstanding both for its insights, its loving wisdom, and its clear, simple instructions for working with angelic beings. I have every expectation that it will become a classic in its field. I recommend it without reservation.'

David Spangler, author of *Everyday Miracles*

'In a moving, candid and funny book, [William Bloom] gives crystal-clear information about the hidden forces that shape our reality, and combines intuition and intellect in opening to the angelic realms. Packed with fascinating anecdotes from his wealth of personal experience, he makes working with angels seem as ordinary – and as essential – as brushing our teeth. Brilliant – I loved it!'

Gill Edwards, author of *Living Magically* and *Stepping Into the Magic*

'Before my own perceptions of the elemental and angel world were clear enough, I got a sense of their presence through William Bloom's teaching and writing. It is wonderful that his new book has such a range of exercises. It is time for everybody to exercise communication with these subtle worlds!'

Marko Pogacnik, author of *Nature Spirits and Elemental Beings: Working with the Intelligence in Nature*

'William Bloom writes clearly and persuasively of parallel worlds which exist side by side with ordinary reality, but which the vast majority of us have been taught successfully to block out of our awareness. He has a unique ability to make the mysterious accessible and understandable. He leads readers far into the subtle realms while making sure we keep our feet on the ground.'

Leo Rutherford, founder of Eagle's Wing School of Shamanic Studies and author of *Elements of Shamanism*

'*Working with Angels, Fairies and Nature Spirits* is not a book that fosters escapism or romance. William Bloom reminds us of the spirit world, and the inherent help, beauty and magic that is available to us in both mysterious and practical ways'

Angeles Arrien PhD, cultural anthropologist and author of *The Four-Fold Way* and *Signs of Life*

'Joyfully easy to read and follow, *Working with Angels, Fairies and Nature Spirits* filled in gaps in my own understanding. William Bloom provides concrete and comprehensive explanations of the world of spirit; and gives helpful suggestions for how we ourselves can contact the angels and spirits. He shows how what seems to be empty space is filled with energetic life – physical, emotional, mental and spiritual – life that is part of a loving and understandable universe, a marvellously coherent universe.'

Dorothy Maclean, author of *To Hear the Angels Sing* and *Choices of Love*

WORKING WITH
Angels, Fairies
& Nature
Spirits

About the Author

Dr William Bloom's teaching about angels is based on twenty-five years of direct personal experience. The founder of Holistic Partnerships and of the Core Energy Management approach to self-development, Dr Bloom is also considered by many to be Britain's leading holistic educator. His other books include *The Endorphin Effect, Feeling Safe* and *Psychic Protection*.

Other books by William Bloom

The Endorphin Effect – A Breakthrough Strategy for Holistic
    Health and Spiritual Wellbeing
Feeling Safe
Psychic Protection – Creating Positive Energies for People and
    Places

WORKING WITH
Angels, Fairies & Nature Spirits

WILLIAM BLOOM PhD

PIATKUS

© 1998 William Bloom

First published in 1998 by
Judy Piatkus Books Ltd
5 Windmill Street
London W1T 2JA

email: info@piatkus.co.uk

Reprinted 1999, 2000, 2001 (twice), 2002, 2003 (twice), 2004, 2006

The moral right of the author has been asserted

*A catalogue record for this book is available
from the British Library*

ISBN 0 7499 1904 3

Edited by Esther Jagger
Designed by Sue Ryall

Printed and bound by The Bath Press, Bath

For Sabrina Dearborn

At certain moments of illumination, the reality of the world becomes apparent, and its glory so magical that you have to cry aloud what you can see of its wonder.

JOHN MASEFIELD

I am not ashamed to tell you what ought to be told – that I am under the direction of messengers from heaven, daily and nightly.

WILLIAM BLAKE, *The Jerusalem*

I am a little world made cunningly
Of elements, and an angelic sprite.
JOHN DONNE, *Holy Sonnets*

Acknowledgements

To all the students on my courses, who were also my teachers. To Frances Howard-Gordon for accompanying me on the first stages of this journey. To the Findhorn Foundation where I was able to teach and experiment. To Sabrina Dearborn for ongoing conversation, inspiration and reality checking. To my mother, Freddy Bloom, a secret animist. To Liz Puttick, my agent, for encouragement and very helpful suggestions on the first draft. To Gill Bailey at Piatkus, who exceeded all expectations with editorial suggestions that were wise and inspired; to Esther Jagger who also nudged me to a much better manuscript and then did some wonderful editing; and to Mel Harrison who kept things relaxed and friendly.

And to all the spirits who have taught and accompanied me.

Contents

Introduction

L ET ME GET this off my chest at the very beginning. You may feel the same way that I do. I have had enough of being thought peculiar because I believe in and work with angels and nature spirits. They are real and their reality is important for us.

I am also tired of writings and conversations about angels that have no awareness of environmental, social and psychological realities. The angelic realm is very beautiful, but it is a beauty that needs to inspire us in the real world rather than lift us into escapist illusion.

The angel world does exist. It is part of the fabric of nature and the universe. It is part of the creative beauty and juice of all life. Knowing this is deeply relevant to the social and environmental problems of our time. It is also relevant to the dynamic need of every aspect of life to fulfil itself. And there is no need for any of us to be embarrassed because we understand and work with the angelic realities.

The purpose of this book is to share clearly the nature of these beings, how we can work with them and learn from them, and why and how they cooperate. I want to marry the mystic experience with some logic and common sense. I want to build bridges in thought, imagination and action between the two worlds, between us humans and the beings of the spirit realm.

For readers who already experience, sense or believe in this dimension, I want to facilitate greater clarity and a deepening of the experience. For readers who know about this dimension because of your interest in myth, archetypes or anthropology, I want to provide a logical explanation which will persuade the rational left side of your brain of their actual existence. I want *Working with Angels, Fairies and Nature Spirits* to bring understanding, common sense and practical help to anyone who is interested in this field.

This is a practical book about practical cooperation with the spirits: I am not describing something that happens simply in the human mind. The flow of the book is simple. The early chapters describe in a general manner how and what spirits and angels are; how we experience them and can cooperate with them; and something of my own history of involvement. The book then goes deeper in understanding them and how to work with them, providing a number of practical exercises to help you gain direct experience.

I began to work consciously in this area almost thirty years ago and then started to hold workshops. As a result this book is written not only from the perspective of my own experience, but also from that of listening to hundreds of other people and being part of their voyage of learning and clarification.

Once when I was teaching a course on spiritual practice I reminded the participants that they could work cooperatively with invisible spirits. I described, for example, how to call in a spirit of the home – a household angel – and explained how the spirit's presence creates a more friendly atmosphere. I heard a gasp, and looked up to see a Japanese man smiling and shaking his head.

'I know all this!' he exclaimed. 'My mother and my grandmother did this all the time. And my grandfather too. Many people in Japan do this. And I had to come to London to be reminded!'

We live in a time when our beliefs are changing. Two hundred years ago, as the Western world began to industrialise and become 'modern', we rightly began to throw out superstition and religious manipulation. But we also wrongly threw out many true spiritual realities which did not fit the scientific view of things. There is an essence of religious folklore which is true, beautiful and creative – even if it cannot be scientifically proved. Elves, muses, angels and similar beings, known collectively as devas or devic beings, belong to this essence.

Japan, although on the surface a sophisticated, technological Westernised society, has retained its connection with such spirits, and the family of the Japanese man in my class performed a small daily ritual to call in and greet their house angel. This is not in fact unusual, and still happens in many cultures all over the world. Before starting their day, people light a candle or make an offering to the spirit of the house, inviting it to be present. Harmony in the home is enhanced and encouraged. The atmosphere really changes.

This simple act of pausing and inviting in a helpful spirit can happen in almost every aspect of our lives. These spirits bring practical benefits: psychological wellbeing, a greater sense of the beauty of life and an easier atmosphere for achieving creativity and excellence. And whether we invite them in or not, whether we acknowledge their presence or not, they exist and they are everywhere.

Understanding this dimension and, most of all, experiencing it can practically and directly enhance our lives and activities – at home, at work, gardening, in business, in the arts, in relationships, in spirituality, and in healing and psychological growth.

My own awareness of angels and spirits, and my work with them, has brought me great comfort, inspiration and enjoyment. I wish you the same blessings – and many more.

1

Our Spirit World:
Reality or Illusion?

IN EVERY CULTURE and in every age there have been people who have recognised, felt and understood the importance of spirit beings. Today, the further you get from urban centres of civilisation, the more likely you are to find people who take spirits and angels for granted. On the west coast of Ireland, the fairy world is a matter of fact in many communities. I remember a very stocky tough farmer, who had worked for years as a labourer on the London Underground system, talking casually about the little people. He had a beer in his fist and might just as easily have been talking about football or farming equipment.

Sceptics: 'It's All in the Mind'

There is a huge body of writing from myth, anthropology and folklore which places these beings purely in the world of the human psyche. Angels and spirits, they state boldly, are of course not real – they are creations of the human imagination.

At the turn of the last century, for example, the anthropologist Professor Sir John Rhys wrote, typically, in *Celtic Folklore, Welsh and Manx* that the origins of fairies were in the demons and divinities 'with which the weird fancy of our remote forefathers peopled lakes and streams, bays and creeks and estuaries'. This is the general attitude of social anthropologists studying tribal peoples and historians looking at classical cultures such as those of ancient Greece or Rome. The invisible beings of a parallel world, the gods and goddesses, angels and spirits, are all, to these scholars, the creations of a fanciful mind.

This is despite the universality of the experience. The great mythologist Joseph Campbell, in the first volume of his series *The Masks of God* points out that when anthropological research from around the world began to be gathered in the eighteenth and nineteenth centuries, something startling became clear. What had been thought of as culturally isolated incidents of spirits and angels were in fact a worldwide phenomenon. Nevertheless academic anthropologists, sociologists and psychologists have largely tended to dismiss the possibility that these parallel beings are real.

Mainstream psychology believes that everything of the 'inner' worlds is the creation of the biological brain, so the slightest discussion of the angel worlds immediately suggests that the speaker may be in need of psychiatric treatment. There is even a psychological theory that the Western idea of angels, fairies and nature spirits is, in the words of the Swedish folklorist C. W. von Sydow, 'a creature of erotic dreams and hallucinations'. Why else should they have such beautiful limbs and rounded breasts? Why are they wearing tantalising transparent clothing? They might possibly be, writes Lewis Spence in *British Fairy Origins*, a 'monument of an early erotic attitude to supernatural beings'.

In *The Erotic World of Fairy* Maureen Duffy quotes from an Elizabethan play:

Ioculo: I pray you, my pretty little fellow, what's your name?
Third fairy: My name is little, little Pricke ....
  When I feel a little girl asleepe,
  Underneath her frocke I peepe.
  There to sport, and there I playe,
  Then I byte her like a flea.

Perhaps the most famous collection of stories about the spirit world is *Grimms' Fairy Tales*. And fairy tales is precisely how they are regarded. In common usuage, when we say 'fairy tale' we mean a story about something that is not real.

So is this whole subject the creation of the human imagination only? Certainly it is that part of the mind which knows how to imagine which helps open us to sensing and communicating with the inner world beings, but these beings are emphatically not projections of naive minds.

There is something terribly patronising and close-minded in the idea that the many thousands of classical, mystical and tribal cultures which believed in spirits were deluded and working purely with psychological imaginings. There is no smoke without fire. The universal experience of these inner worlds points to a reality that cannot be dismissed.

The Presence of Daimons

We live in a world where we are not brought up or educated to relate to these invisible beings as real. Nevertheless the most cynical materialists often sense a magical presence accompanying a plant, a tree, a river, a waterfall, a mountain or some other aspect of nature.

'I didn't want to tell anyone,' a builder once said to me, 'but I could definitely feel something. Working in the garden, there was something there, some kind of presence, but I didn't want to say anything in case people thought I was soft.'

With less embarrassment, the explorer Sir Francis Smythe, who climbed Mount Everest, said that he felt accompanied by a presence on the final stages of his journey. 'In its company I could not feel lonely, neither could I come to any harm. It was always there to sustain me on my solitary climb up the snow-covered slabs.' As the Irish poet AE (George Russell) wrote, 'The Golden World of invisible beings is all around us ... beauty is open to all and none are shut out from it who will turn to it and seek it.'

Artists and mystics, by their very nature, are also at the fringes of civilisation and they often feel deep and important relationships with the angelic realm. In the twentieth century England's

most noted woman mystic poet, Kathleen Raine, has been very
open about her relationship with her angel, her inspiring muse,
whom she calls a 'daimon'. 'I cannot remember', she once wrote,
'when I was not aware of the presence of my own daimon'; and
she also described her relationship with it in her poetry:

> *Long ago I thought you young, bright daimon,*
> *Whisperer in my ear ...*
> *But now life in its cycle swings out of time again*
> *I see how old you were,*
> *Older by eternity than I, who, my hair gray,*
> *Ever dim with reading books,*
> *Can never fathom those grave deep memories*
> *Whose messenger you are,*
> *Day-spring to the young, and to the old ...*

Every day many people experience this subtle feeling of some
other presence being close, of being certain that they have met an
angel or spirit. Over the last few years there have been a number
of popular books, films and television programmes on this theme.
One of the most significant is the American prime-time series
Touched by an Angel, whose episodes focus on people in a
distressed psychological state who are helped by a small band of
angels.

My own favourite true story of this kind is from some friends
who were camping in a remote forested area. About 3 a.m. they
were woken by a voice telling them to get out of their sleeping
bags and move the tent. It was so clear that, despite the effort,
they did just that. Towards dawn, a huge fir tree fell and crashed
on to the exact spot where their tent had previously been.

Of course these can seem to be just fairy tales and, to the
sceptic, mean nothing. But how many of these types of story have
to be told before sceptics will open their minds?

The Need to Suspend Disbelief

The experience of spirits is not due to electrical communications
between our brain cells. The spirits exist in their own dimension

with all the reality with which we ourselves exist in our dimension. And they intertwine invisibly but intimately with the world that we can see and touch and feel. Far too many people have ongoing, very real and enjoyable experience of this other world for it to be other than an objective reality.

Those who refuse to be persuaded are reminiscent of the reception given to the medieval Venetian travellers returning to Italy with news of China. Nobody believed them at first. The Venetians, and Europeans in general, thought that theirs was the only civilised world. In particular they thought that through Christianity they had reached a peak of cultural excellence. The travellers who returned from the East told of a fabulous civilisation with wonderful buildings, scientific inventions and a degree of social sophistication that the West had not even dreamed of. It was of course all true, but the narrow-minded Europeans could not believe that such a culture existed. Only after several other travellers had confirmed these reports were they given credibility.

How many people have to report on the reality of the angel world before today's closed minds open?

Re-enchantment: Learning from Tribal Cultures

Many people today are also aware of the need to re-enchant our culture, to regain the sense of mystery and magic that belongs to a healthy society and to a healthy creative human life. The genius of modern science and technology are undeniable, but we also need to reclaim an appreciation of the depth, complexity and beauty of life. This will bring us back into a more balanced relationship with the world – one that encompasses curiosity, respect and gratitude. It is a fundamental requirement if we are to re-create a healthy environment and sound ecology. And it is also poetically healthy – food for the soul and the flesh.

Re-enchantment will enable us to regain our feeling for the life and consciousness that is in everything – rock, plant, lake, animal, mountain, planet, cosmos. It is not so difficult to sense the inner life that sparkles and plays through nature.

This inner and invisible dimension includes the world of

spirits, who are connected to every aspect of life, including our human thoughts and actions. This is a renaissance of the natural religion of animism – recognition of and respect for the life and spirit in every single aspect of nature and the universe.

Almost without exception, small tribal communities who live in a close relationship with nature believe in the spirits that animate all aspects of life. Such a belief is found among native peoples in the Amazon rainforests, on the plains of North America and the Steppes of Siberia, in the icy wilderness of the Arctic, on the African savanna and deep in the Australian desert. They recognise, for instance, that plants, forests and other places have spirits, and that it is appropriate to honour these spirits. Therefore they regularly conduct ceremonies in which gifts are made to them. The native American ceremony of smoking a pipe of peace and blessing, for example, is always accompanied by presenting some tobacco to the spirit of the place. In Western society the tradition of throwing coins into a well or fountain is a modern continuation of respecting these spirits. Equally, many of us will still not visit someone else's home without bringing a gift.

In tribal cultures there are also special people, often called shamans by modern commentators, whose role it is to communicate with and understand these spirits. In the Amazon rainforest, for example, these shamans take a natural herbal narcotic, iawaska, which helps them enter into an altered state of consciousness. In this trance-like state they open up and are able to fully perceive and communicate with the important spirits.

In fact, according to tribal lore, to be separate from the spirit world denies us a full experience of life. To embrace this parallel dimension is not naive or superstitious, but fulfilling, holistic and practical. It stimulates ideas and is a source of creativity. It also confers responsibility for our environment and fellow creatures.

That there is a world of spirits and that we can work cooperatively with them is a commonplace in tribal traditions. Members of these societies claim that their fundamental survival and quality of life are based on a healthy relationship with the spirits, and find it extraordinary that modern civilisation ignores them.

Devas and Spirits

In Hindi and the ancient oriental language of Sanskrit one word is used as an umbrella term for all the different types of spirits and living patterns: deva. There can be a deva of something as small as a blade of grass or as large as a planet. Devas work both with the living things in nature and with the inner world of concepts, thought and inspiration. There are, for example, devas of justice, of good communication and of religious ceremony.

All across the Indian sub-continent and eastern Asia, millions of households begin their day by pausing and making an offering to the spirit of the home. Built into the rhythm of life is an ongoing acknowledgement of the devas. It is an irony that, as modern educated Asians begin to reject all this as superstition, we in the West are again beginning to honour and understand its importance.

TERMINOLOGY

In the English language we can easily use the word 'spirit'. We talk about the spirit of a place or a dance or even a car. In this context we all understand that we are talking about the essence and inspiration of something. So throughout this book I use the words 'spirit' and 'deva' interchangeably. 'Angel', 'muse', 'living pattern' and 'blueprint' (see below) also carry the same meaning.

We use many words for the different kinds of spirit: elementals of earth, water, air and fire; fairies and gnomes; cherubim and seraphim; angels and archangels; archetypes; muses, gods and godlings. In semi-scientific language, there are also blueprints or morphogenetic fields. This is the idea that atoms, cells, rocks, plants and animals have an energy field which contains the memories of their experiences, a topic which will be discussed later in the book.

That there is an invisible spirit to all living things is a common understanding in mystic and tribal religions. Trees, mountains, lakes, animals, rocks, household objects, buildings, plants, rivers, dances, rituals, healings, communications, gifts – the list is endless – all have an invisible spirit. This deva dimension is part of the creative matrix of everything that exists.

Some of these beings are so magnificent that they have been described as gods and goddesses – the spirits, for example, of great mountains of cities or astrological constellations. Others are tiny and make up the elemental life of a microscopic particle of rock or the most minute drop of water. The mystic and tribal traditions teach us that these spirits can influence and inspire us to our and their benefit.

ANCIENT TRADITIONS ACROSS CULTURES

Students of esoteric mysticism have long studied these invisible spirits and in some traditions, such as the Jewish Qabalah, the Christian Gnosis and Tantra, there are clear maps and descriptions of their different types and kind, from tiny elemental salamanders and undines, through fairies and cherubim, to muses, great archangels and dragons. In the nineteenth and twentieth centuries the teachings of anthroposophy and theosophy, based respectively on the ideas of Rudolph Steiner and Madame Blavatsky, have also attempted to describe and explain the whole geography of the inner and metaphysical worlds.

Classical civilisations openly recognised that there were spirits who inspired and guided the various aspects of human culture. The pre-Christian gods and goddesses of Rome and Athens can be understood as great devas. Names such as Mercury, Ceres, Neptune and Venus still have great charisma and archetypal power. In classical Athens it was acknowledged that there were devas who inspired education and the arts; there were, for example, the nine muses – Calliope, Clio, Erato, Euterpe, Melpomene, Polyhymnia, Terpsichore, Thalia and Urania. Again, there were special priests and ceremonies specifically dedicated to communicating with these spirits and to providing a channel for their expression. This parallel dimension is also referred to by some of the great philosophers, particularly by Plato, who wrote about perfect forms – pure ideas that float around in an inner dimension and which contain the perfect blueprint of their earthly companion.

In analytic, depth and transpersonal psychology, there is also some understanding of an inner dimension, separate from the individual mind, yet accessible to all, in the idea of archetypes. Carl Jung's theory of archetypes is the beginning of an appreciation of these deva realities. In this kind of psychology, there is an acceptance that people can be affected by outside influences that exist beyond the usual psychological history or everyday realities.

CEREMONIES AND RITUALS

Even today most religions still have fabulous and moving ceremonies that explicitly work with angels. There is, for example, the famous Christian invocation for 'Angels, Archangels, seraphim and cherubim, and all the heavenly company' during Holy Communion. C.W. Leadbeater's book *The Science of the Sacraments* contains a moment-by-moment description of the angelic cooperation that takes place in Christian ritual. In Tibetan Buddhism, great clanging symbols and horns call in the devas of purification and of prayer. Mohammed himself was inspired by an angel of divinity.

It is often recognised still that the great harvest festivals of most cultures – in spring for sowing, and late summer for harvesting – are not hollow invocations for help or expressions of a job well done. They are clear calls to the spirits of nature and landscape to enhance fertility and growth, and to maintain continued cooperation.

One of the most magnificent deva ceremonies that lived on into the twentieth century, and will almost certainly be repeated in the twenty-first, is the coronation of the British monarch. In this long and extraordinary rite all kinds of symbol, ritual and invocation are used to invite in and crown the new monarch with the blessing and inspiration of all the different spirits. These spirits include the *Volkgeist* or folk soul of the United Kingdom (see p. 51), the spirit of regal authority and the spirit of justice. The crown itself is a symbol of higher wisdom, an invitation to the angel of divine intelligence. This whole crowning in fact only makes sense when understood as a rite to connect the monarch with the relevant inner spirits who will overlight and be able to inspire him or her during the reign. Similarly, many parliaments start their day with prayer or silence, an invocation for guidance from the spirits of government.

Repression and Revival

Throughout history the great religions and, later, the process of industrial modernisation have tended to repress this awareness of the spirits. Sometimes this repression was cruel, involving torture and death. Many women were accused of witchcraft and burnt alive purely because they loved plants and their spirits. Sometimes just being playful in nature was enough to incur condemnation. In 1634 Mary Spencer was condemned for rolling her bucket downhill and running with it. There are many theories as to why a religion dedicated to love and turning the other cheek should have become so harsh and vindictive. But whatever the reason, the fact is that for several centuries the Christian Church conducted a horrifying campaign against anyone who disagreed with its doctrines.

This meant that any woman – or, indeed, man – who had a sense of the beauty of nature and its inner life was an immediate target. The very word 'witch' still has the connotations of evil imposed upon it by the Inquisition, when 'witch' in fact has always meant 'wise woman'. A woman, therefore, who was aware of the spirits of plants or of the home was immediately condemned as, in the words of one priest, 'an evil liver; a social pest and parasite; the devotee of a loathly and obscene creed ... a member of a powerful and loathsome obscene creed ... a member of a powerful secret organisation inimical to Church and State'. The word 'paganism' also has negative connotations for many people because of Church repression and hostility. In fact 'pagan' merely describes someone who honours the spirit and spirits in all life.

People need to be realistic about the extent of this repression of women and natural animist religion. In the two centuries from 1500 the English authorities alone were responsible for the deaths of thirty thousand women. In Europe one Lutheran prelate, Benedict Carpzov, condemned twenty thousand to death. The exact numbers tortured and killed cannot be accurately estimated, but the words 'holocaust' or 'genocide' are not out of place. Up until the last century, Christian missionaries were still killing people in South America for their animist beliefs. Psychologically, missionaries are still terrorising pagans – people who respect the beauty and interdependence of life. This religious fundamentalism against spirits and women can also be found in Islam and Judaism.

Huge shadows of this psychological and physical oppression remain. Ironically, organised religion and science, usually in ideological conflict, both sneer at the belief in fairies, elementals, gnomes and all the other spirits.

HEALING THE WOUNDS

But today, as we pass through another stage of great cultural change, into a planetary village of free communication, we are resurrecting our relationship with the spirits. This is partly due to a simple freedom of information. Nobody is going to be burnt or tortured any more for talking about spirits, and the wisdom is freely available in books. We also feel more free to talk about our experiences, and the reality is that many people do indeed experience spirits.

We also have a psychological and emotional need to resurrect them and honour them. Ignoring them is part of our contemporary disease of cultural imbalance. Their repression may well be linked with two other great social wounds. One of these is the disrespect and repression of the female dynamic. Too much power lies with men and male attitudes, and it desperately needs to be balanced by a new respect and status for women. The hijacking of leadership and influence by a male-dominated culture has created disastrous imbalance. There are, of course, healthy signs that this is being healed.

The second wound is the conflict between humanity and nature, the abuse of our environment and ecological relationships. Over the last two centuries in particular our species has developed a selfish and thoughtless attitude to our environment. The damage caused is in turn hurting us and our children. There is a beautiful native American Ojibway prayer that expresses this situation:

> *Grandparent,*
> *Look at our brokenness.*
> *We know that in all creation*
> *Only the human family*
> *Has strayed from the sacred way.*
> *We know that we are the ones*
> *Who are divided*
> *And we are the ones*
> *Who must come back together*
> *To walk in the Sacred Way.*
> *Grandfather,*
> *Sacred One,*
> *Teach us love, compassion, and honour*
> *That we may heal the earth*
> *And heal each other.*
>
> Quoted in Andrew Harvey (ed),
> *The Essential Mystics*

We are, thankfully, beginning to learn again that we are creatures of an intimately interdependent universe, and that we are fully responsible for an environment that can support us or let us sink into oblivion.

But there is also a third wound which many people feel is just as deep and harmful. It is the lack of cooperation between humanity and the spirit world. We are only now starting to recognise this wound and the need for its healing. The huge fascination with angelic phenomena and other paranormal events, and the new respect for tribal religions and shamanism, are an indication of the instinctive need for this connection.

A recognition of this sphere, letting its influence into our minds and behaviour, stretching to cooperate with it, can bring about a further deep balancing and healing. It will bring us a true spiritual wealth to feed our psychological poverty. It will balance our obsessive 'doing' with a more harmonious 'being'.

2

Tuning In and Feeling the Effect

W HAT IS OUR purpose in working with spirits? What do we hope to achieve?

Education, Practical Aid and Inspiration

Our aim in doing so is far more than just an attempt to add quality to our activities or to be more successful in our lives. Its essence lies in the education, the service and the spiritual growth that come with the experience. When a gardener feels accompanied by nature spirits, or a priest senses an angel of ceremony, or a shopkeeper senses some presence in her shop, or a healer feels the vibrations of a healing angel – in all these situations education, practical aid and inspiration are offered.

When Kathy, a nurse, consciously calls in a healing angel to help her with a patient, she knows that she is bringing in a companion who fully understands the subtle flows of energy that are often needed in healing. When Craig, a gardener, tunes into the nature spirits before laying out a new flower border, he knows he is getting advice that genuinely creates a more beautiful and productive landscape. At a very practical level, the difference between a gardener who is attuned to nature spirits and one who is insensitive is immense.

A personal and spiritual transformation also comes from working with spirits. This happens because we have to slow down, centre, expand our awareness, fine-tune our discrimination and act with sensibility. These are key elements of spiritual maturity. When John, a company director, attunes himself to the spirit of his business, he slows down his normal frenetic pace and relaxes his usual need to control. In connecting with the spirit of his business, he is able to perceive and understand his work in new and creative ways.

The Benefits

Compared to light or sound or cosmic waves, we human beings live in very dense and constrained physical bodies. Through our five major senses we connect with and perceive the material world around us. The noisier, the bigger, the more colourful, the smellier that something is, the more do we notice it.

We trust these five dense physical senses, and have more trouble with our sensitivity to more subtle realms. The inner realm of the spirits is not physically obvious. It does not shout in our faces like a television or speeding car. Yet when we choose to give this inner realm some attention, its reality is overwhelming. It is the same with nature. Some people never notice the beauty of our environment, whilst others live permanently nurtured by and in awe of it.

Accepting the existence of a world of spirits expands the whole way that we make sense of and experience life. Without chaining us to any particular belief system, it provides us with a religious experience of life – religious yet without religion. It gives us magic and poetry, and a deep appreciation of the underlying intelligence in all life.

THE IMPORTANCE OF REALITY

But practicalities must also be borne in mind. We live in a real world that is full of suffering and injustice. All of us, to a lesser or greater degree, endure this. And many of us, to some extent, feel a calling to engage with the suffering and work for a better world. But to rely purely on human resources for our support and inspiration does not seem enough. To survive successfully, to engage meaningfully in personal and social change, it helps to have a sense of connection and inspiration from the other companions in life.

Just knowing they are there brings a cosmic twinkle into even the worst situation and can provide much-needed strength. More than that, understanding how and why they exist, and knowing how to connect with them, brings fantastic support into our lives. How often have you wanted inspiration or wisdom for what you were doing? The devas will give it to you if you give yourself enough time and openness to receive it. And if you do choose to begin to work cooperatively with them, you will begin to change the whole mood and atmosphere of your life.

In modern times, however, many people fear that an interest in spirits can detach us from reality and support fantasy. (I remember lecturing on devas once to an audience in New York where two people in the front row genuinely thought they were elves and kept nodding strange encouragement to me.)

But there need be no disengagement from reality. This work expands our awareness into a greater reality without losing our grounding in the here-and-now. It attunes us to the essence of what we are doing, to bring us fresh inspiration. All of this is good for us, for nature and for the world. Henry Beecher, a Protestant minister, expressed this well in his *Royal Truths*: 'There's not much practical Christianity in the man who lives on better terms with angels and seraphs than with his children, servants and neighbours.'

First Connections

Our first cooperative connections can most easily be made in the pause before any activity. Many people do this instinctively. As they pause before beginning some aspect of work, they may concentrate or enter a kind of day-dream mood. They seem to be changing mental gear, getting into the right 'state'. Then, when they have an instinctive sense of being prepared, they begin.

Something interesting, exciting and subtle happens when we make that pause. We are orienting ourselves. We are getting ready for the activity and building up an inner idea of how we want it done and how we want it to be when finished. We are taking stock of the situation. We are drawing consciously and subconsciously on our own memories, past experiences, wishes and intentions.

THE INVISIBLE BLUEPRINT

But something else is happening too. It is almost as if we are waiting for a wave of inspiration. Subconsciously and telepathically, in that pause we are also connecting with the pattern or blueprint of the activity we are about to do.

For the moment, just accept the hypothetical idea that every activity has its own plan or structure. For the moment, also accept the notion that this pattern or blueprint is alive in its own right. This 'inner' invisible pattern is made of subtle energy and has a life of its own. We can also call this pattern the 'spirit' of the activity.

The pause may be only a few seconds, or it may last months or even years. But however long the pause, that is the time when people are connecting with the inner pattern, the spirit, of their work.

- Leonardo da Vinci pauses before painting the Mona Lisa.
- The cleaner pauses before scrubbing the kitchen floor.
- The architect pauses before drawing.
- The gardener pauses before pruning.
- The mechanic pauses before taking out the engine.
- The lover pauses before touching and caressing.

This may be the biggest conceptual jump that some people have to make. It is easy enough to sit beside a tree or a mountain and feel that there is a presence, an energy, there – but not so easy to accept that human activities also have this inner spirit.

When Leonardo paused before painting, the genius of his own consciousness and creativity was coming into relationship with the spirit of painting, the muse of the style of art. In the same way you or I, about to clean the kitchen or fix the car, can attune to the spirits of those activities.

Some readers may well feel sceptical at the idea of a deva for clean kitchens! But this can be countered in two ways. First, looking at our cosmos of emerging, exploding and imploding galaxies of stars in infinite space, it is already pretty bizarre that on one tiny speck of a planet little two-legged creatures with cloths and cream-cleaners are scrubbing away at sinks! As the cosmos consists more of energy and consciousness than of physical matter, it is more likely to find an energy and essence connected to the activity, than the activity itself. Second, consider all the homes around the world, especially in India and China, where there is a small shrine in the kitchen. It does not take much imagination to sense that the aura around this altar really encourages and supports the cleaning and other household rhythms.

There are indeed spirits to help us in everything.

Ancient Boat-Builders' Rituals

This natural human process of pausing before an activity and tuning into its spirit was turned by many tribal societies into an ongoing continuous ceremony. Domestic life and work were entwined with a ritual acknowledgement of the spirits. Even today, the boat-builders of the Trobriand Islands in the South Seas still provide a wonderful example. They build their ocean-going canoes as a continuous ceremony of calling in the appropriate devas to help them construct the perfect vessel.

The spirits of the ocean and of past boats are called at the very beginning and asked to guide every part of the construction. Before the islanders go into the forest to cut the tree that supplies the main hull, they talk to the spirit of the forest and ask it to guide them to the perfect tree. They sing to the spirit of that tree before felling it.

As the boat is carved out of the trunk, songs and rituals are performed, calling in the devas of the ocean to help them make the boat ride the waves smooth and fast – a friend of the waves, the ocean and the beasts of the deep. When the prow of the canoe is carved, a specific spirit is called in to help the boat dance on the water and cut it cleanly.

Even in the industrialised world we still name our ships and bless them with champagne before sending them on their maiden voyage. Only a few hundred years ago most large ships still bore figureheads – spirits carved on their prows to call in good fortune.

Turning work into an ongoing ceremony of communication with the relevant spirits is commonplace in tribal cultures, but academic anthropologists usually only perceive superstitious behaviour and rituals for social bonding. Primitive peoples, it is explained, pretend to control that which is uncontrollable. But this is a blinkered understanding.

For the tribal boat-builders the ceremonies are part of a careful technology in which no chances are taken. The spirits, the living inner patterns, guide the boat-builders in their work, ensuring cooperation at every stage from the elements and good fortune. The spirits guide the builders in constructing the most perfect boat of which they are capable. These living ideas, the spirits of the wood, of the ocean and of the waves, are the best possible counsellors and consultants.

Hsun Tzu, a Chinese sage who lived approximately three centuries BC, said:

> It is through rites that Heaven and Earth are harmonious and Sun and Moon are bright, that the four seasons are ordered and the stars are on their courses, that rivers flow and that things prosper, that love and hatred are tempered and joy and anger are in keeping .... He who holds to the rites is never confused in the midst of multifarious change .... Rites – are they not the culmination of culture?

Cooperating with Spirits Today

This kind of active cooperation with the spirits is not restricted to so-called primitive peoples. It exists on many levels even in modern Western society.

IN THE GARDEN

For instance on one of my courses Veronica, a businesswoman in her thirties, talked about how she gardened.

'Before I prune my rose bush, I watch it for a while and just stand by it. It's as if I'm warning it about what I'm going to do. At the same time I'm catching the sense of how best to do the pruning. Then when I cut, it doesn't feel so harsh. It feels more cooperative. I'm not doing it *to* the plant – I'm doing it *with* it. I feel as though I'm doing it in cooperation with the ....' She paused as she realised what she was about to say. 'I feel as though I'm doing it hand-in-hand with the *spirit* of the bush.'

'Don't you worry about making mistakes? Or hurting the spirit?' someone asked.

'I did when I first started gardening,' she replied, 'but over time I became more confident. I became more attuned to the plant spirits.'

IN BUSINESS

Then there was a Scandinavian who, unclear about his business's next stage of growth and prompted by his wife, came to my course on devas. This was not perhaps the most obvious place for a businessman to seek help and advice.

'I was educated in classical history and I have always enjoyed mythology,' Sven explained. 'In the roots of our Western civilisation there was a time when these mythical beings were part of everyday life. Even the trading markets had special gods. I have this sense that my business could also have its special god, its special spirit or angel.'

After the course Sven returned to Scandinavia and a year later he described what had happened. He had begun to go into his office very early, before any of the staff arrived. He would light a candle and go into a quiet and contemplative frame of mind. After considering his factory and all his workers and contracts he invited into his quiet time the angel and spirit of his business. Then he would sit quietly for a while, seeing what thoughts and images passed through his mind. He was pausing before work, attuning to his business and to its spirit.

Over the next few months he took certain very clear actions which came from the thoughts and images of his quiet time. He had trees planted at the entrance to the factory. He changed the lighting in the main work areas. He closed the executive dining room so that both workers and management ate together in the main canteen.

These were just the first of many decisions which were inspired by his morning attunement with his business deva. He did not put into action every thought and whim that passed through his mind, but acted on those which were appropriate, made sense and appealed to his gut instinct. Over the following months the unions became increasingly cooperative, productivity soared and he himself found a new quality of life in his work.

He might perhaps have reached similar strategies from bringing in a management consultant, reading a book on Feng Shui or perhaps just listening more carefully to his workforce. But the truth for him was that all of this came out of his willingness to attune to and connect with the muse of his business. His decisions came from his own wisdom and attunement. This was deep and important work for him, both practically in his business and in his own psychological growth towards integrity and inner peace.

It is clear from this businessman's story that working with devas not only helps practically, but also changes the style and atmosphere of activity. Life is lived with more awareness and a greater sense of connection and calm.

IN RELATIONSHIPS

Another example of cooperation comes from Jane, whose marriage was falling to pieces. She knew that if she and her partner's lovemaking could become more harmonious and satisfying it would go a long way towards healing their relationship. So she sat in silence and contemplated their lovemaking. She invited in the inspiration of Eros, the winged cherub of love.

As she sat quietly, several clear ideas passed through her mind which she later put into action. She bought a candle, dedicated it to romance and the healing of their relationship, and let it burn overnight. She waited for an evening when there was plenty of time and then invited her husband to help heal their relationship. She lit another candle asking in Eros and an angel of healing. And their relationship did begin to heal.

Again, you could say that she could have adopted the same course of action and helped her marriage if she had followed the advice of a friend, or a counsellor, or her own common sense. But would she have felt the same quality of invisible support, and would her husband have been so easily persuaded?

Sometimes the effects of calling in a deva can be dramatic and immediate. Anne was having terrible trouble with the people in the house she shared. There were continual rows and the atmosphere was most unpleasant. After learning how to call in a home spirit, she went home and cleared a small space on a shelf in the kitchen. On it she placed a flowering plant and a small candle.

'I light this candle,' she said, 'to call in an angel for this household. Thank you for your presence and for your love. Thank you for being with us to guide and inspire us to become a cooperative household. Thank you for your presence.'

She said that the atmosphere improved overnight and stayed that way.

Having read these people's stories sceptics might suggest many psychological reasons for these kinds of changes. But I have studied psychology for thirty years and, like many mystic psychologists, I know that there is a dimension beyond it. Cooperating with this spirit dimension can have truly wonderful effects.

3

A Personal Journey

T HIS SUBJECT IS not a theoretical or philosophical one for me. One of my aims in this book is to share with readers some of my direct experiences, in the hope that my own journey may help to explain more about the spirit world and how we can communicate with it and benefit from it.

It all began in my late teens when I became fascinated by altered states of consciousness, mysticism and the occult, and read widely in these areas. By my early twenties I was meditating and undergoing psychoanalysis with an analyst who had worked with Sigmund Freud. I was working at the time in book publishing and was an activist in community politics.

A Chapel in the Mountains

In 1970 I came across a peculiar book called *The Sacred Magic of Abramelin the Mage*, which described a six-month ritual whose purpose was to achieve full conversation with one's 'holy guardian angel' and to contact various spirits. The ritualist had to build a small chapel and go into isolation for six months whilst conducting this ceremony.

I was strongly attracted, even though I was not sure whether guardian angels or spirits really existed. I thought that they might perhaps be hidden aspects of my own psyche – psychoanalysis and meditation had made me aware that there were hidden parts of my mind, psyche and emotions. To 'invoke my guardian angel' and then meet some spirits seemed a perfectly sensible way of taking forward my inner exploration. This would be just another way of discovering these concealed layers of myself.

So my partner and I left our publishing jobs in London and disappeared into the High Atlas mountains of southern Morocco. We found a small hunting lodge that had been built by a Frenchman fifty miles south of Marrakech and three miles off the nearest road. At six thousand feet, in winter we sometimes had six feet of snow; but in the summer we would look up and see golden eagles soaring overhead. There was neither electricity nor running water, so we used a local well, candles and oil lamps. We stayed there for two years.

The Ceremony

I built the required small chapel and began the daily ritual of prayer and invocation – reflecting on my past, asking for forgiveness for past wrongs and then asking to meet my guardian angel. Not really knowing what I was doing, I threw myself into the spirit world when I committed myself to this intense ceremony of the Western mystical tradition. I was twenty-five years old and those six months fully opened the doors of my perception into the world of devas, angels and spirits.

Four months into the ritual, most of my day was spent in prayer and contemplation, reading and walking in the valley. My diet was vegetarian and I slept on my own. Strangely, I had found no difficulty slipping from the rhythms of city life to those of asceticism and devotion.

Not surprisingly, I began to enter into a different state of awareness. Like many people, since childhood I had from time to time sensed that everything was alive. Trees, plants, clouds, animals, rocks, landscape – all had a vibrant quality. But now the peak experience of feeling and seeing the throb and beauty of life in everything was with me all the time.

Psychologically, however, I felt distressed and anxious much of the time. But I was comforted by the companionship I now received from the landscape. Everything in it was a friend. It was so satisfying that I found human companionship, by comparison, complicated and confusing.

In the final weeks of the six-month ceremony I was on my knees up to six hours a day, telling God my faults – not unlike psychoanalysis – and asking for forgiveness so that I might be pure enough to have communion with my guardian angel – not at all like psychoanalysis. It was a very intense period, and nothing in my social or educational background had prepared me for it. A very charged atmosphere was also building up around the home-made chapel.

I went into it on the day of the ceremony's climax and lit the oil lamp and the incense. Kneeling before the altar, I began to pray with great intensity, asking for communication with the angel. Nothing happened. I continued to pray fervently for communion with the angel. Still nothing happened.

Desolate, confused and hardly able to walk, I staggered miserably back into the house and threw myself on to my bed. I began to weep, and then fell into a strange sleep. My body relaxed and my mind surrendered. Suddenly a voice in my head seemed to wake me and call me back into the chapel.

I did as instructed and knelt, dejected and pathetic, before the altar. And then I began to feel the presence of great beauty.

Something invisible was there. I experienced a wide and expansive energy field, warm and forgiving, hovering over and in me. It loved me, and was unlike anything that I had experienced before. It was a specific and real being. With its support, in the following days I called in and met other spirits. And since that time I have experienced an ongoing and conscious involvement with the deva world.

Reflection and Integration

The spiritual path, it is said, has its own wisdom that may often surprise us. Directly after the six-month ceremony I collapsed with hepatitis and was forced to slow down completely. Whether I liked it or not, I slowly had to integrate the experience of those six months. I was seriously ill for six months and convalesced for another eighteen. At one point I was virtually paralysed for several weeks as no oxygenated blood was circulating through me.

But looking back, I sometimes think that without the illness I might have gone mad. I was very young and very intense. The illness forced me to mellow and took me into a process of reflection and integration.

What Was Real?

During those long hours of contemplation my sceptical, inquisitive mind looked hard at the events of those six months. Were they delusions? Or pure imagination? But always I came back to what I had actually experienced and not to how my educated mind tried to rationalise it. Even if I could not explain the events in a logical, coherent way, the reality was that I had felt and experienced this invisible world. It was there as an undeniable experience, as clear as the wind blowing branches and the water flowing down rivers into the sea. I had opened my awareness permanently, and I could not ignore it even if my rational mind doubted it. And the truth was, and is, that I loved the reality of the spirit world. I felt completely comfortable with it. It made me feel good, more alive, more connected to all life.

Staying in the Real World

Because of this deeper sense of connection, this new awareness did not separate me from human life. I was not looking to escape from the 'real' world. In fact I came back to England, did postgraduate work and then began to teach.

My ability to sense the spirit world would melt away, however, if I was emotionally or mentally intense, if I was very tired or had been drinking alcohol. In all these states I closed down and was too dense and 'armoured' to sense the inner dimensions. But as long as my lifestyle remained reasonably stable I could feel the deva world as easily and clearly as I could see and smell a rose. It was there, and I was open to it.

Nor did this awareness of spirits make me into some kind of spiritual adept or saint. I was still the same kind of person I had always been, challenged by the same psychological patterns: I often describe myself as a calm neurotic.

My need for personal change reinforced my desire to maintain my sensitivity and to explore the deva world more deeply. I found the inner world very beautiful, and felt myself in need of this balancing beauty. Experiencing connection with the deva world put me into a more intimate and sensitive relationship with nature and supported me, giving me the strength to be honest with myself in my psychological journey and healing. But perhaps most important for me was that my awareness of the spirits gave my life a deeper quality and enjoyment.

Teaching What I Needed to Learn

But I was not clear what these devas and spirits actually were, nor did I fully understand how best to cooperate with them. So I embarked on a long period of experiment, research and education. I read many of the books listed on p. 161 and was particularly inspired by a Tibetan teacher, Master Djwahl Kuhl writing with Alice Bailey, in particular *A Treatise on Cosmic Fire*. This book grounded my awareness of how devas work not just in the world of form and nature, but also in the realms of emotional, mental and spiritual energy. It also helped me to stop trying to understand them as being like humans. I began to recognise that they possess a consciousness completely unlike ours, and to realise that I needed to stretch my imagination and mind to encompass their true nature.

HEALERS, GARDENERS, RITUALISTS, ARTISTS
AND BUSINESS PEOPLE

I also began to teach courses on devas. It is a truism that teachers teach what they need to learn, and this was so for me. I have learnt the most from listening to and understanding the experiences of my students.

I taught my first deva course in summer 1983 at the Findhorn Foundation in Scotland. This is a relaxed and innovative educational spiritual community of several hundred people; they have a general acceptance of devas, in particular those that work in nature and with plants. Beforehand, I felt somewhat anxious: what kind of strange people would sign up for such a course?

But at our first meeting the group of students seemed absolutely normal: fourteen women and ten men between the ages of eighteen and seventy-six. There was only one woman in diaphanous purple silk, and she was a painter. The rest included a computer programmer, a secretary, a priest, a carpenter, a businessman, a doctor, a social worker, a pagan and a sales assistant. As each person introduced themselves my caution melted. They were mature working people, all of whom had had experiences which they wanted to clarify. The essence of their experience was a distinct sense of cooperation and inspiration coming from another dimension. They wanted to understand what had been happening, and to work more effectively with it.

From this first course came some startling insights that simplified so much of the subject. All the participants were interested in household angels, but to my surprise they naturally divided into five very distinct groups – a pattern repeated at all my subsequent workshops:

- *People working in healing and caring*: healers, doctors, nurses, teachers, social workers, counsellors and therapists.
- *People working with plants and landscape*: farmers, gardeners and horticulturists.
- *People working with ceremony and ritual*: priests, nuns, priestesses of the Wicca tradition (the modern religion of witchcraft, as opposed to the 'black magic' kind), shamanic students, freemasons and ritual occultists.
- *People in the arts*: painters, writers, architects, musicians, poets, designers, architects and creative workers in general. This group also sometimes included mathematicians, computer programmers and engineers.
- *'Business' people*: office workers, entrepreneurs, lawyers, manufacturers, publicists and marketing professionals.

I think of these five groups as healers, gardeners, ritualists, artists and business people.

Different Categories, Similar Approaches

In the many sessions that followed, an obvious guideline for working with spirits began to emerge. It had never previously occurred to me that there would be a similarity between the approach of an ordained priest and a gardener, or between that of a healer and a business person. But, in fact, all these categories did work in a similar way. These people all appreciated that some invisible and subconscious help was available. They therefore always paused before any activity to allow this help to come close. Most of them – in different ways – asked for this help to come in.

Out of this understanding emerged two clear stages for cooperating with spirits, which will be explained in greater detail later. The first is attunement and the second is invitation. As I looked back over my time in the mountains, I saw the whole six-month ceremony as essentially this process of attunement and invitation.

ATTUNEMENT

Before any activity, take some time quietly to tune into both the activity and its spirit. Stop for a few minutes, become calm and quietly contemplate the activity you are about to do. At the same time relax and open yourself to sensing the essence or spirit of the activity. Many people do this instinctively – what may be new is to do so consciously.

INVITATION

While you are in the gentle and open state of contemplation and attunement, communicate an invitation to the spirit. In whatever way works for you, silently or spoken, call in the spirit. Then – and this is very important – thank the spirit for being present with you as if it were already there.

The Fallacy of the 'Third Eye'

While teaching the first workshops, a very simple insight emerged about how most people perceive and sense spirits. Mystical lore is full of confusing information about clairvoyance and the 'third eye', an invisible organ of perception that sits towards the centre of the forehead. It is claimed that you have to be at an exceptional stage of spiritual advancement for this third eye to function properly. When it does, the theory goes, you will be able to see, in technicolour, all the inner beings and energies.

But from my own experience and that of many other people involved in this work, I realised that the classis description of how the third eye works is only partially accurate. The more general truth is that we all have energy fields, an electromagnetic aura, and we sense when something comes into our energy field. Our mind-imagination then interprets the sensation.

The vast majority of us do not see clear images or hear distinct sounds. Most of us actually feel and sense changes in the atmosphere, subtle moods, new vibrations in our energy field. To expect clear visual images may be naïve and disappointing for you. The real trick is to notice what you are feeling in your own field. This process will be described in greater detail later.

Spirits as Blueprints

A third major insight emerged from these classes: that devas are the inner patterning for all aspects of life. Contemporary science has trouble understanding how it is that the energy, particles and waves bind together to become coherent atoms. The missing substance is the deva of the atom, which fulfils two functions. The deva is an energy pattern or blueprint of how the atom should be. It is also magnetic, attracting and 'gluing' all the energy, particles and waves into the form of the actual physical atom.

These functions of holding the pattern or blueprint and magnetically attracting and bridging the elements into form are what devas do in all aspects of life. The spirit of a plant precisely holds the pattern of the flower and attracts it into that form. The spirit of a ceremony does the same for the different elements of the ceremony.

So although spirits live in a parallel dimension to ours, that dimension is totally interwoven with and necessary to ours. To understand and work with spirits is not to take a trip into another realm, but to expand our awareness about the nature of life and living here and now. It is indeed a separate dimension, but any assertion that it is irrelevant is to miss how central it is to the whole matrix of life. Holistically, devas exist in exactly the same reality as us. Their mode of consciousness and activity, however, is fundamentally different from ours.

Devas in the City

These insights about the nature of devas were not purely intellectual: my practical experience of spirits was continuing too. To my surprise, even in the city it was easy to perceive the vitality and magical life force that surrounded plants and trees. The dancing energy of plant and landscape spirits stands out against the monotone of tarmac and concrete. Walking into any public park or private garden, it was obvious how vibrant the inner energy was. Pausing briefly, it was very easy to feel the devas.

In fact, in a public place such as London's Kensington Gardens there is fairy lore as rich as that found in any Tibetan valley. Next to the playground in the north-west corner is a tree trunk filled with fairy carvings lovingly restored by the comedian Spike Milligan. Alongside the Serpentine lake is the famous statue of Peter Pan with its willowy, elfin figures. Christine Hartley, a well-known occultist, warned me once of the spirits that lived in the roots of some of the great trees of Kensington Gardens. She said they had a sombre and depressing vibration that frightened young children and those of a nervous disposition. Only recently, after the death of Diana, Princess of Wales in 1997 an area of the park became a huge floral tribute, as spectacular an invocation of spirits as could be seen anywhere in the world.

Ritual and Ceremony

It is not just parks and open spaces that house spirits. The angel ecology of cities in general is as fabulous as that of any rain forest. Huge devic activity focusses on religious ceremonies in churches, temples and other places of worship. Our twentieth-century cities experience the same spirit involvement as in tribal or pre-Christian religious rituals.

Having discovered this, I became attracted to organisations with a strong sense of ritual: the Christian Church, with its celebration of Mass, Eucharist or Holy Communion, and a particular order of freemasonary which had included Krishnamurti, one of the most influential spiritual teachers of the twentieth century, among its members. In the Catholic and Orthodox traditions in particular, a profound magic takes place within the ritual. In fact, some mystics have described the Eucharist as the supreme ceremony of Western culture. And when the masonic ceremonies were performed correctly, the temple became a kind of magical, sacred theatre with an atmosphere that sparkled. Performing these rituals over and over again gave me the time and space to sit quietly within them and contemplate their energies and atmospheres.

Insecurity and Delusion

At this time I took a formal course in social anthropology, which is mainly the study of tribal peoples, and came face to face with academic hostility to the idea of a spirit world. I was, of course, particularly interested in the rites and religious practices of these tribal peoples, but the academic interpretation was that all the rituals and relationships with spirits were merely projections of the mind which, in one way or another, served psycho-social needs. In other words, tribal peoples were hopelessly naive and, insecure in the face of uncontrollable elements, had created this imaginary universe which enabled them to delude themselves that they could control their environment.

My own father, a Freudian psychiatrist, shared this attitude and could never bring himself to face the truth that I had spent two years in Morocco on a spiritual retreat to meet my guardian angel. It was more comfortable for him to think that I had gone abroad as a tax dodge! Here indeed was a projection and a fantasy to give him psychological security. In fact, the general hostility of academics to spirits is a sign not of their wisdom, but of their insecurity in the face of a reality which they cannot control or understand.

Western civilisation has only recently begun to stop patronising the 'primitive' mind and the imagination of children. At last we are beginning to realise that the repression or dismissal of the primitive and childish imagination is not an indication of maturity and civilisation. It is, rather, the loss of one of our greatest assets – of being in creative communion with the joy and spirit of all life. To begin to understand spirits we need only to reclaim our natural instinct for animism.

Ironically, it was during this period, when I was in daily contact with academics who still thought in the old ways, that I had a very powerful and unexpected experience of city spirits.

The Angel of London

I had been looking at old maps of London and learning about its shape and history before the fields and forests, valleys and hills had been overwhelmed by buildings. Then one morning as I was cycling to college, I suddenly felt myself connected to a very beautiful presence whom I knew to be the spirit of the city, the angel of London. I had not really thought of London having her own angel, but as soon as I felt the connection it seemed obvious. In classical times all cities, towns and villages had their guardian spirits or gods. It seemed that she wanted to guide my journey and show me certain places. I could feel her presence so clearly in my energy field and my mind–brain easily accepted what seemed to be her messages or guidance.

For the next few months she guided me around London, pointing out the flow of the landscape, showing me various natural energy centres and also telling me which elements of city planning and pieces of architecture she liked. She took me to small gardens and parks, sometimes nestling behind churches, which I had never known before. It was wonderful to feel the forces of nature amongst the bricks and mortar of the city. She also took me to places of worship and education and entertainment where she appreciated the particular flows of energy.

I was sometimes surprised by her preferences. Her favourite spot was the crescent on the north bank of the Thames at the centre of which stands the Egyptian monument known as Cleopatra's Needle. She enjoyed the way in which everything was placed in relation to the flow of the river. On the other hand, again to my surprise, she did not like the famous Nash Regency terraces of Regents Park, partly because they blocked the natural flow of earth energy from Parliament Hill and Primrose Hill down into the city, and partly because they involved no healthy flow of human life.

She also introduced me to the healing angels which overlight even the largest, most hi-tech hospitals and work with them. 'The hospitals may appear harsh,' she seemed to say, 'but sense the healing energy that exists in them. Walk the wards at night and feel the healing care. Much of this channels through the staff. Patients and carers are drawn towards fulfilling patterns of perfect healing. This is held there by the healing angels.'

One spring morning I felt called by her at dawn to Primrose Hill, an ancient site where druids still perform ceremonies and which boasts a spectacular view south over London. It was the morning of a full moon and I was up on the hill before the sun rose, sitting in meditation, waiting to sense whatever it was that she was going to show me.

As the dawn crept into the sky I could feel the usual fresh flow of vital energy that begins to move across the landscape as the first light of the sun begins to turn the darkness grey, then white and finally clear. Then I began to feel the angel doing something of her own. It was as if she were lifting up and expanding the whole of her energy field to draw in as much of the dawn's vital energy as possible. Her movements were slow, long and magnificent. Then I began to feel the flow that was coming through her, as enormous floods of vitality were pushed through the city and directed into all the natural life which inhabited it. The life-force flowed into trees, shrubs and plants everywhere, into the parks, gardens and back yards, into the small window boxes, into the weeds growing in the cracks of pavements. Pets and all the animals in the city, including the human beings, also absorbed the gift. The movement through her energy body lasted perhaps twenty minutes and then gently subsided.

'Magnificent,' I communicated. 'You do this at every full moon?'

'No, no, sweet boy,' came the reply. 'I do it every morning.'

My experience with this spirit opened me fully to the idea and reality of city angels, who were an everyday part of most classical cultures. It is impossible to think of the roots of Western civilisation as being in Rome and Athens and then to ignore their city deities.

Repairing the Fairy Ring

As well as encounters with the city devas I continued to experience devas of landscape. Let me end this chapter with an almost classic tale of an encounter with nature spirits, which illustrates how a purely energetic experience is irresistibly translated into archetypal images.

When my son was small we lived in a cottage in the country. Every day I would put James in a carrier on my back and the two of us, along with our dog, a collie called Blue, would go walking in the nearby woods. In one part of these woods my attention was often drawn to a holly tree whose overhanging branches formed a small dome about eight feet across. The earth beneath was bare, and there was a magic quality to this small space.

Anyone who walks in the countryside knows that there are special places which have an atmosphere of playful magic. Sometimes these spots are circular and bordered by a ring of fungi. In British folklore they are often called fairy rings. Underneath this holly tree was what looked and felt like a fairy ring, now overgrown with weeds and brambles. Walking past it one spring day, I received the clear impression that I was being asked to clean it up. This impression remained with me every time I walked past it, but I never did anything about it.

Summer arrived, and I still did nothing. By Autumn I began to feel some remorse, even shame. Finally I took some clippers on our daily walk. James was just about able to sit up, so I propped him up with a twig in his hand and then crouched down to enter the fairy circle.

Both child and dog left me in peace as I clipped out all the overhanging creepers and cleaned up the dome under the holly tree. I cleared the earth of all the old stones, branches and rubbish until the dome and circle looked perfect again. In fact there were two fairy circles, one about eight feet across and to its side another about two feet across. I had cleared up the physical reality to match the inner pattern.

It had taken me half an hour to do the job, and miraculously James, who was only sixteen months old, had sat there happily all the time. Who or what, I wondered, had been entertaining him? I picked him up and we stopped for a few moments of meditation focussing on the fairy ring. I apologised for taking so long to do it and for the fact that the job was not perfectly done, but hoped that it might in some way serve as a token that at least one representative of humanity was alive to the deva realm.

The next day I took James and Blue out again for our normal walk. Suddenly I became aware of a large amount of very playful activity in my energy field. The whole path and surrounding area were filled with chirping and dancing deva energy. It seemed that there was a procession waiting to lead us along the path towards the holly tree. It was a procession of gratitude and celebration.

My mind could not help but project images of little folk with acorn hats and wispy pink creatures with shimmering wings. Flowers and grass stalks were held up like flags, and they played strange little stringed instruments and trumpets and drums. The whole wood seemed to resonate with the fun of the occasion.

When we reached the holly tree it seemed that there was a formal and rather solemn vote of thanks given to me, and I was embarrassed at their gratitude because I had delayed so long over such a simple task. But they were thankful for the human involvement.

They then dressed me in green tights with curling elfin shoes, a jerkin with tassels, special green gloves and a green hat. They dressed baby James in a similar outfit but did not give him a hat, so I asked why.

'He will only receive a hat,' they replied, 'when he himself has done something for us. He has the eye for us, but he will have to actually do something as well.'

We watched as they performed circle dances in the fairy ring and tiny baby fairies danced in the smaller second circle. Later a procession led us down off the hill.

As James grew up I took him to different places with a magical atmosphere and talked to him about this event and about nature spirits in general. He grew up to be a tough young man, but he kept his energy field open and could sense them quite easily. When he was sixteen he came to me one day after a weekend visit to the countryside.

'I have my green hat now,' he told me, explaining that he had cleaned up another fairy ring and felt them come to him with gratitude.

Sometimes when I am travelling in foreign countries I feel the devas of the landscape coming out to take a look at me because they sense that I have a working relationship with them. They hover around discussing whether a cosmopolitan Western man could be able to work with them.

'Oh yes I can,' I say to them.

'Prove it,' they respond.

'I have nothing to prove,' I assert. 'Look at what I'm wearing.'

And they see my green outfit which belongs to the elves and fairies of England, which of course was originally called Angel-Land, and these foreign nature spirits believe me. But they still like to see proof of cooperation – so I do something for them.

Of course there are people – especially sceptics, cynics and scientists – who would like me actually to prove everything. Unfortunately they cannot see my lovely elfin outfit. They could, however, see the certificate for my PhD in political psychology. I value my doctorate and my elf suit equally.

4

Invisible Companions
throughout the Universe

THIS CHAPTER STARTS by taking an introductory look at the different kinds of spirits and the intriguing question of what they really look like.

Another interesting question is what we look like to them. How do they experience us? Perhaps we are just colours and sounds to them. Perhaps they feel us in the atoms and molecules that make up our system. Perhaps we are energy systems like Russian dolls. I imagine that to them we are as natural a creation of universal life forces as anything else in the cosmos. We are as fascinating, as dynamic, as natural as the complex ecology of a rain forest or the flows of wind and cloud in a weather system.

There is a wonderful quotation from Alan Watts, the Western teacher of Zen, which expresses how human beings are natural. 'We do not "come into" this world; we come out of it, as leaves from a tree. As the ocean "waves", the universe "peoples". Every individual is an expression of the whole realm of nature, a unique action of the total universe.'

Animism, Energy Fields and Unseen Partners

It is easy for most people to imagine that a flower has an invisible partner: the scent and radiance of the flower lead us to this point and its energy field is almost tangible. But this energy field is not just a radiance that emerges from the physical plant – it exists in its own right, as a being in its own dimension, and it holds the blueprint or pattern for that flower. It is the spirit or deva or fairy of the flower.

As the seed grows to become a sprout and then a green plant and later a flowering plant, the deva is always there with it. Throughout the plant's growth, the deva holds around the plant the energy pattern for its growth.

Not only the plant world has this invisible partner. Every aspect of life – mineral or vegetable, animal or human, tiny or cosmic – has its inner, invisible companion that carries its energetic blueprint or pattern. Everything that exists, both seen and unseen, has within itself the idea of what it is. These ideas are actual living beings inhabiting a parallel and intertwining universe. As explained in Chapter 1, throughout history and in many cultures there have been animist religions based on this concept.

What Do They Really Look Like?

Since devas span a huge range of beings from the spirit of an atom through to that of a planet – tiny elementals to great archangels – they are obviously not all the same, no more than a pebble is like a tree or a snail like a giraffe. They are also energy beings without dense physical form.

Although they are not human, it is very normal for us to anthropomorphise them – to give them human characteristics – which is a natural part of how our mind–brain understands life. We clothe spirits, who have no solid form, in images of people in order to accept them more easily. In fact, it seems almost impossible to think of a spirit without projecting a human image on to it.

The next two chapters focus on the ways in which we sense and perceive devas. The most important point, however, is that we sense these beings in our own energy field and our mind–brain seeks to interpret this sensation by projecting an image on to it.

Like everyone else, though, I have been very curious about what they really look like, and once spent some months regularly contemplating this question, trying to feel and see the patterns of their energy bodies. The impression I kept receiving was that of a dancing double spiral of energy with a canopy of strands extending from it, like a jellyfish with the body of a vortex. Other people have had the same image.

In an earlier book I stated with certainty that this double vortex shape was what devas looked like, and that it varied only in size and vibration. Ten years later I am not so confident, and wonder whether I was clothing my experience with the famous image of the double helix shape of the DNA molecule – part of the chromosomes which carry the genetic information and blueprint of how the body of a plant or animal is going to develop. There are also many other natural spirals in the universe, including the shape of galaxies. On the other hand, all these spirals might well be reflections of the energy bodies of devas.

In general, though, people's images of a spirit usually correspond with its overall vibration or feel. The energy pattern of a flower, for instance, is small and delicate. When people feel or tune into that energy pattern, it is not surprising that they project on to it the image of a small female dancer.

SAME SPIRITS, DIFFERENT IMAGES

All across the world, culture by culture, the same types of spirit are given different images. A visit to any anthropological museum will reveal the richness of these variations. Consider, for example, those nature spirits which work with plants, animals, and the landscape. In Europe they are often clothed with an image that is half-human and half-goat – fauns, satyrs and Pan. The Hopi people of North America see them as feathered cochinas, half-human and half-eagle. In many African cultures they are perceived as wood, leaf and straw creatures, half-human and half-plant. These are all the same spirits, but clothed in images relevant to the local culture.

In classical Mediterranean mythology these spirits are envisaged as fauns who evolve into Pan figures, half-goat and half-animal. Such landscape spirits can be found in almost every culture the world over. Their appearance in myth reflects the way in which each culture relates to its native plant and animal life – eagle beings, figures of 'green men' covered in foliage, wood and leaf spirits and so on.

Sometimes this human tendency to clothe a sense with an image also extends to imbuing it with a sound or smell. When sensing flower spirits, many people hear tinkling noises. Some of the muses and ceremony devas are often portrayed as carrying musical instruments – harps and flutes and trumpets – reflecting a tendency to 'hear' them as well as 'see' them (as, for instance, in my own fairy ring experience described at the end of Chapter 3). The mind–brain may also project impressions of a smell. When I have invited a faun-type spirit into my teaching groups, its members often catch a musky odour of animal and organic material.

There can also be a very clear sense of size. It is obvious that the spirit of a mountain is going to be very large. When I ask groups to tune into the deva of a tree, they frequently feel that the spirit's energy body is much taller than the tree. In an exercise we do when a Pan spirit communes with a group, people often receive the impression of a being twice the height of an average man.

What can clearly be stated is that devas are energy beings without solid form, but perceived by the various human cultures in certain ways to suit a particular culture. It is also certain that, because of the power of consistent human thought, some of the devas may absorb into their energy bodies the imprint of the human projection. If people think and project, for example, the image of 'fairy' enough times, it can create the clothing of a fairy. But the actual form is still dancing energy.

Let us look now at the general sweep of angels and nature spirits which occur frequently in the experience of most cultures.

Elementals

The tiniest devas recognised by humans are the elementals of earth, water, air and fire. These are the beings that help to hold together the fabric of the material world.

EARTH

The earth elementals are usually imagined as little dark-coloured creatures with squat bodies and flat faces, carrying buckets and spades. The Walt Disney film *Snow White* contains a classic image in which the seven dwarves are seen working away in their magic crystal mine.

The atmosphere around such beings is often dense, contracting and uncomfortable, so there has been a tendency to think of earth elementals as dour and grumpy. Goblins, gnomes and hobgoblins all have this kind of character, but the feeling of sombreness comes from the way we experience them in our own energy fields, when our vibration is focussed down into dense matter more than usual. It is as if the force of physical gravity has created a corresponding mood of emotional gravity.

In many cultures these earth elementals have developed into fabulous beings such as dragons and mile-long earthworms which move deep in the earth along the energy lines and cracks in the crust. The dragon with its flaming breath is one image of the huge, powerful earth elementals connected with earthquakes and volcanoes. The great mythic earthworms are the huge nature spirits who care for the invisible energy network of the earth. These creatures ride the ley lines, the earth's equivalents to the meridians and energy lines of acupuncture in the human body.

WATER

It is spectacularly easy to feel the magical deva life of water, especially when it is moving. Here are the elementals of water, the undines, swimming and swirling and diving. Wells, streams, waterfalls, rivers, lakes and oceans are full of these beings. Places where there is water, perhaps in the form of a stream or well, often become regarded as holy, and shrines are built there or offerings made to their spirits. Many of these wells, such as the Chalice Well in Glastonbury, are considered to possess healing spirits. Unknowingly people still make offerings to these spirits when, for example, they throw coins into fountains.

It has also long been recognised that rivers have angels inhabiting them. In India the Ganges, for instance, has an indwelling spirit so pure and powerful that the river itself is considered a god. The city of Benares on its banks has three miles of temples, shrines, pavilions and towers. The Nile and Euphrates, among others, are also perceived in this way, and offerings are often made to them. Even today, people who are sensitive to landscape spirits regularly throw gifts into London's Thames, once famous in Europe as a holy river and called after the Egyptian goddess Isis. Archaeologists working here have discovered evidence of huge rituals in which gifts such as ceremonial swords, chalices and shields were thrown into the river.

The alluring playfulness of these water spirits in the sea is mythologised in the tales of mermaids. Here we have a perfect anthropomorphisation of an energy flow, with the image of her flowing fish's tail, alluring body and long silken hair, singing hauntingly to sailors. But the ocean also has far more powerful water beings, such as Titan and Neptune.

AIR

Sylphs and air spirits are always to be seen and felt in breezes and explosive winds. People see them dancing in the moving leaves and wisping through the cloud formations which they speed through the sky. In European Romanticism the sylphs are the most clichéd of fairy angel girls, in diaphanous clothes and with silken wings. Sometimes this cliché extends to fat cherubim with puffed up cheeks blowing through fluffy white clouds.

Air spirits are also recognised, in larger form, as the gods of weather, carrying and pushing the currents of climate around the earth. At the top of totem poles across North America can be seen the eagle-nosed god who works with weather, the Thunderbird. All around the world, humanity has sought to connect with these spirits because of their tangible effect on weather and agriculture. Shamans often lead tribal rituals to influence them.

I have several friends who have been taught how to work with these air spirits and occasionally ask for their cooperation when, for example, they are taking a group out to work in landscape. One of them went into meditation at Findhorn to ask for a sunny afternoon on a specific day. He came out of the meditation slightly bemused but smiling. 'I have the impression,' he said, 'that someone else has been working the weather. I don't think I can get what I want.' Sure enough, we found out that a visiting Native American teacher had that morning performed a weather ceremony.

FIRE

Is there anyone who has looked into a fire and not been fascinated by the fire elementals, the salamanders? The flames are living creatures. Imagine the beings who are the essence of these flames. The scope is enormous, from the tiny beings of a candle flame to the grandeur of the sun. In their most magnificent form they are the spirits of the fire and heat in the centre of the earth, and the angels of fire which burn within the sun. More gently, have you ever considered why the lighting of a candle, when done with some quiet intention, is so magical? Almost immediately there is a new atmosphere. Go into the places of worship of almost any religion, and you will find lamps and candles burning, flickering communion with the spirits of fire.

There is a wonderful meditation exercise which simply involves contemplating the inner spirit of the sun. What is probably the oldest-known prayer, from the ancient Hindu tradition and known as the *Gayatri*, is addressed to the sun and hints at an awesome dimension of deva reality.

> *O Thou Who givest sustenance to the universe,*
> *From whom all things proceed*
> *To Whom all things return,*
> *Unveil to us the face of the true Spiritual Sun*
> *Hidden by a disc of golden Light*
> *That we may know the Truth*

And do our whole duty
As we journey to Thy sacred feet.

The Natural World

PLANTS

The best-known devas are those that accompany every plant, from the tiniest wild flower to the greatest redwood. Have you every lain flat on the ground and looked through the grass of a lawn or meadow? In this fascinating microscopic world there are also tiny beings. If every atom has its minuscule deva essence binding it together, so too does every little plant have its spirit. More than that, each bud and grain and flower has its own tiny magical energetic companion. The theosophical writer C.W. Leadbeater likened these minute devas to ants and bees.

When people say that nature spirits are only to be found in special places, they have no real understanding of them. Wherever there is a weed or strand of grass growing between two bricks, there you will find fairy life. In your window box or garden, in the trees and plants that grow in city streets and by busy motorways, there are plant spirits. They deal with the harsh intrusion of human civilisation in the same way they deal with the raw force of the elements. We are just another part of nature, sometimes hard and aggressive, at other times cooperative and helpful.

As soon as the root system of a plant becomes substantial, new devas work with the interaction of plant and earth, and with the absorption of moisture and minerals. These beings are partly earth elementals and partly nature spirits, and are often depicted in myth as brownies and goblin types that lurk around trees playing in the roots and grumbling. Again it is because of their 'earthy' feel that this sombre and withdrawn image has been projected on to them. Although this may seem peculiar, they like people to jump up and down on the strong roots of their trees. It seems to set up a tickling vibration which they find amusing and pleasant.

The trees, of course, have very ancient accompanying spirits that overlight and envelop them. In their energy field and awareness they hold the history of all that has taken place in and around them. This can sometimes feel poignant as well as beautiful. Chapter 8 explains how to heal this sadness.

SENSING THE SPIRIT OF A TREE

Stand close to a tree and let your awareness go down into the root system where it absorbs nutrients from the earth. Follow the flow up into the trunk, the branches and then the leaves. The leaves are open to receive the light of the sun. Hold your awareness of the whole tree and then expand your focus slightly to be aware of the whole energy body of the tree. Stay quietly with this sense of the whole tree, and its spirit may become quite clear to you.

Amongst tribal societies the Hidatsa of North America, for example, believed that the spirit of the cottonwood tree in the valley of the Upper Missouri held magical powers. Resting under it would bring special powers and abilities. According to the anthropologist Sir James Frazer, the inhabitants of Siaoo in the East Indies believe that at the full moon certain tree spirits walk about. They have big heads, very long legs and arms, and ponderous bodies. In order to keep them quiet, the local people bring these spirits offerings of food.

ANIMALS

Every individual animal also has its accompanying spirit, but more important in human mythology has been the greater spirit who holds the pattern for the whole species. There is, for example, an angel for bears, another for eagles, and so on. There are also angels for all the breeds.

Many people, particularly in deliberately induced trance states, meet these animal spirits and learn from them new attitudes which are useful in human life. Certain tribal and clan groups feel aligned with specific animal spirits, and the lifestyle of that animal spirit offers very helpful ideas on how to behave and survive in their particular environment. I return to this subject later.

LANDSCAPE

These spirits have evolved so that they now understand the perfect ecological set of relationships for a stretch of landscape. They hold the blueprint for all the interdependent plants and creatures.

There are also highly sophisticated landscape angels which understand not only the ecology of the local flora and fauna, but also the way the earth energies work in a particular place. They can be found at all the great sacred sites. They work particularly with the way the forces of vitality and fertility flow into and through the earth, and carry patterns which aid the fulfilment of all beings within their aura. Recognising their presence and the power of the landscape, people have often built temples and devised ceremonies to create a relationship with them. Such places exist across the world and include Glastonbury in England, Jerusalem, Mount Kailas in Tibet, Mount Shasta and the Niagara Falls in North America, Harare in Zimbabwe, Ayers Rock in Australia and Lake Titicaca in Bolivia.

Glastonbury, the 'Isle of Glass', also known as Avalon, was reputed to be the capital city of the angelic beings. The centre of druid worship, it later became the home of the greatest abbey in Christendom. Even today residents and pilgrims from many belief systems perform rituals there, from the making of corn dollies to honour the spirits of fertility through to Christian pilgrimages and processions.

Also attracting pilgrims from different faiths, Jerusalem has unfortunately become a place of bitter religious conflict. Different beliefs and rites compete dangerously with each other for predominance. This is a terrible paradox – a place so filled with angels that the eagerness to worship there has created a rivalry that is often fatal.

HUMANITY AND CIVILISATION

Many spirits accompany the 'natural' environment and it is the same in the human world. Tribal and animist religions never conceived of human beings as separate from nature or the spirit world. We too are accompanied by a host of spirits, an army of angels.

To understand the spirits related to humanity, it is crucial to appreciate that thoughts and feelings, in their own dimension, have as much reality and substance as a plant or an animal or a mountain. Just as there is solid material, fluid material and gaseous material, there is also material that is emotional and mental. When you think or feel something, the energy you have put into that feeling continues to exist.

This emotional and mental energy is bound together by devic essence in precisely the same way that an atom of solid matter contains devic essence. There are wave particles of emotion and mentality, just as there are wave particles of earth and water.

There are, therefore, many types of spirit whose major realm of existence is not in solid physical life but in emotion and thought. This can also, of course, be said about people. We do not need physical bodies to be emotional and mental beings.

Because human beings are so active emotionally and mentally, we create a whole world of feelings and thoughts filled with spirits. As always, the spirits are carrying blueprints of perfect fulfilment. Those that accompany humans are benevolent and helpful. By their very nature they are attuned to how we can best fulfil our potential. They do not experience the kind of friction that we do as we pass through time and space.

This idea of an inner pattern of perfection into which we can grow is the underlying theme behind all ideas about guardian angels. They are not detached beings who intervene in crisis, but constant companions who always hold us in their aura. These guardian angels are perfectly attuned to who we are in essence, who we are as souls.

At various times in our life, when we are ready for change or it is forced upon us, we may suddenly have an awareness of these accompanying spirits. It is no wonder that they are imagined as being like us, but more magnificent, with golden radiance and wings that lift us to heaven. In other traditions, however, these companions may be pictured as animals or dragons or other beings who bear no resemblance to humans.

These spirits are aware not only of the potential of individuals but also of our group activities and aspirations. As mentioned earlier, millions of families around the world have household altars to honour the spirit of the home. These are spirits who understand the harmonic that can be achieved in a family and a home. And there are also, of course, spirits who understand the dynamics of love and relationship. Cupid-Eros is well known as the deva of perfect love between a couple.

Certain spirits accompany our activities, such as the angels of healing and the muses who inspire our creative endeavours. Others understand the ideals of humanity – these are the spirits of justice, compassion, democracy, education, art, architecture and worship.

Beyond that there are angels of towns, cities and nations. In classical times every settlement of any size had an altar or temple dedicated to the local angel or god. The idea of nations having an angel of their own, the folk spirit or *Volkgeist*, became particularly popular in nineteenth-century Romantic philosophy and a bastardised version of it was incorporated into Nazi dogma. These folk spirits, it is suggested, manifest themselves in the temperament and characteristics of nations, and are often imagined in clichéd form such as the cockerel of France or the eagle of the United States.

Their origin is in the totems of tribal peoples, all of whom knew that their small tribe or clan was looked after by a particular spirit. The title of the popular book *Clan of the Cave Bear* is based on that understanding. The development of larger and more complex settlements never destroyed this idea of a village or city or people being looked after by its special spirits. The image of these spirits could be manipulated by political and religious leaders in an attempt to influence their following, as attested by the various images given to the English folk spirit. St George, for example, wore armour, slew dragons and overlit medieval English armies going into battle. Britannia sat regally over the British Empire and the Royal Navy's control of the oceans.

THE PLANETS AND COSMOS

The concept of the indwelling pattern or spirit can be extended throughout the cosmic system. If a mountain can have a spirit, why not a planet?

In the art and science of astrology, the constellations of the Zodiac were known to have great angels whose vibrations could deeply affect humans. Many mystical traditions describe the hierarchies of spirits and angels that dwell throughout the cosmos. Theologians and mystical philosophers have contemplated the great angels and spirits who accompany different levels of consciousness, the planets, the sun and the other stars, constellations and galaxies. For example, gnostic Christianity, the Qabalah, alchemy and esoteric Hinduism all offer diagrams and maps of these great entities and their accompanying spirits. In the West, the best-known angelic hierarchy is that described by the sixth-century Greek writer Dionysus of Aeropagite. In descending order it runs: seraphim, cherubim, thrones, dominions, virtues, powers, principalities, archangels and angels. In the 1980s the Vatican issued an edict confirming the existence of angels and asserting that they were the messengers of God.

The contemplation of the cosmic spirits was, however, dry stuff compared to the work of the mystics who sought actually to come into communion with them. At one time academic investigation entered into a strange philosophical debate about how many angels could sit on a pinhead. White magicians, on the other hand, wanted to speed their spiritual journey through experiencing the vibrations of these grand angels. They did this through ceremonies which called in the angels so that the magicians could fully experience them. The ceremonial religion of ancient Egypt, for example, used this approach. Later, the increasing power and intolerance of Christianity and Islam forced its practitioners to go underground. Their rites were perpetuated through the secret orders of the Knights Templar, the Rosicrucians and

Freemasonry, and also survived in the practice of natural witch-craft.

There is a classic, almost caricature, scene in which this work is done. First, a magic circle is drawn to keep out all foreign vibrations and influences. Then the magician brings into the circle objects, colours, scents and plants, all of which are associated with the desired angel. Then, in a state of deep contemplation, the magician attunes to all these objects and invites in the presence of the angel.

You can perhaps imagine one of these great experimenters wishing to commune with the angel of the planet Mars. Within his circle he might have the following objects: something coloured red, something made of iron (the symbol of the planet), some particular plant and some specific scent. All these objects would help him to connect. Then, perhaps with a special verse or incantation, he would ask the angel of Mars to be present. In the vibrational connection, the mystic might then learn great lessons about strength, masculinity, force, dignity, courage and so on.

A Different Culture

So much for the types of spirit and the different images with which the human mind clothes them. But what are they really like?

I would be very cautious about claiming that I know what it is like to be a deva. I am not inside their experience, any more than I am inside the experience of an electron or a wave in the ocean. Nevertheless I know what they do and how they do it, and I am also free to enter their experience imaginatively.

ACTIVE AND PASSIVE STREAMS

The first thing we can note is how different they are from the life-stream with which we are normally familiar – our solid organic world full of activity and movement and change. Look at the difference, for example, between the life of a flower and the life of its fairy. The flower's life is full of activity and forceful energy. It starts as a seed within which a sprout grows and has to crack out from the casing. It then has to push up through the earth, break into the air and stretch up towards the sun away from the force of gravity. It erupts into flower and distributes its seed before returning to the earth for another cycle.

The flower fairy, on the other hand, remains more or less the same. In its field it holds the energy pattern of the perfect flower. Whatever happens in the growth of the flower the fairy remains the same, overlighting the flower and drawing it towards perfection. It does, however, absorb into its pattern the experience of its flower. In this way, partnering its flower, it gains experience and wisdom. So a fairy would have no function or purpose without the plant. The intimate intertwining creates what we see as life.

All the way through nature and the universe this is the general pattern. In the weave of creation, one stream is active and the other passive. But this passivity is very creative. Without the deva and the angelic element, the active stream would spin into chaos. It is the deva which throughout the universe 'bridges' the activity into coherent form. This bridging may not be moving much energy; nevertheless it is a steady hum in the background which calls everything to inevitable fruition.

This, of course, is what is so mystical and divine about the angel world. It is never lost in the strain and stress of the energetic activity of growth and change. Its dimension is always connected to the hope and fulfilment of existence.

A Bridge to Create Form

An atom is the smallest portion of matter in the universe. It contains particles and waves but there is also something that binds them together to create solid form – its deva or elemental. The elemental holds in its field the vision and pattern of the fulfilled atom, and without it the waves and particles would have no coherence.

What the deva elemental does for an atom is what devas in general do throughout the universe. This is their major role, to provide the energetic fabric to create form. Dorothy Maclean wrote in *The Findhorn Garden*:

The physical bodies of minerals, vegetables, animals and humans are all energy brought into form through the work of the devic kingdom. Sometimes we call that work natural law, but it is the devas who carry out that law, ceaselessly and joyfully. *We do not see things as you do, in their solid, outer materialisations, but rather in their inner life-giving state. We deal with what is behind what you see or sense, but these are interconnected like different octaves of the same melody. What we see is different forms of life.*

That form can be a tree or waterfall or flame. It can be a set of ideals, such as justice or democracy, or a healing or a ceremony or any piece of work. To sum up:

- Devas give the material world its pattern and coherence.
- The material world – minerals, plants, animals, humans and human action – gives the devas purpose and activity.
- The deva world and the material world interweave to create our reality.
- Without devas the material world would have no coherent fabric.
- Without the material world, devas would have no purpose.

Through this understanding it is clear that devic essence, the spirit world, is not some rare and distant species or phenomenon, only to be encountered by mystics in trance. As the 'glue' of everything, the spirit world is everywhere.

The Form of Sound

The creation of sound and music provides a wonderful illustration of how devas create form. It is the devic element which bridges vibrations into the form of sound.

Imagine an orchestra in full swing but with no sound. Vibrating reeds in clarinets and oboes. Vibrating lips on brass trumpets and trombones. Vibrating strings in violins, cellos and basses. Vibrating surfaces of drums and cymbals. All these activities are creating vibrations which move in waves through the air and resonate against your eardrums to create more vibrations. But where does the sound come from? What gives the vibrations the *form* of sound? How does the vibrating air hold this wonderful form which we know as sound and music?

To experience this directly, pucker your lips so that you are ready to whistle. You can vibrate the air with a careful blow. But something wonderful gives this vibration the form of sound. The activity of the vibration is bridged into the form of sound by deva essence. The invisible devic fabric takes the intention of sound and gives it form.

Being and Doing

In *A Treatise on Cosmic Fire* by Alice Bailey, the Tibetan teacher Djwahl Kuhl writes that devas see sound and hear colour. And in comparing humans with devas, he suggests that humans have to learn to expand awareness and be, whereas devas have to learn to focus and do.

Let us imagine that devas are communicating to explain their existence:

When we express ourselves within the structure of a single atom, we are the glue that holds the wave-particles, the spin, in material form. Within ourselves we know the perfect structure of that atom. We know its fullest potential. We have in our awareness a full experience of the perfect atom.

Without our presence nothing would hold together.

Our way of life is always to hold in our awareness, in our energy field, a full experience of how an object or being or event could be, if perfectly fulfilled. We experience the potential and its completion.

To fulfil potential, to come to completion, the being has to go through some process of activity. We do not provide any of the power, movement or energy to achieve fulfilment. But we know what fulfilment will be like – and we hold this sense, this blueprint of a fulfilled potential.

We hold this blueprint as a framework to inspire and into

which the being can grow.

We engage with complete affection in this process.

The dynamic that moves an event or being to fulfil its potential is as essential and as wonderful to us, as love is to you.

The Evolution of a Deva

There is a natural stream of evolution in our world which runs mineral → plant → animal → human. There is a similar stream of evolution in the deva world, which might, for example, run elemental → gnome → elf → faun → cherub → seraph → angel. With that in mind, here is a possible life story.

It begins a long time ago with some carbon atoms that were originally part of a tree, but due to earth movements and the passage of time were now submerged a thousand feet down in the earth. These carbon atoms were, like all atoms, made up of subatomic particles and devic essence.

Over thousands of years, and under intense pressure from the weight and shifts in the earth, these atoms slowly changed their molecular structure and form. They turned from wood to peat to coal and then to diamonds. The basic atoms were still carbon atoms, but their form had changed. As their form changed, so did the consciousness of the devic essence which was there from the beginning when it was first part of the carbon in the tree.

The deva absorbed the patterns of its changes and held in its own energy field the new blueprints of the gradual transformation from organic matter to diamond. But when this carbon deva expanded its awareness, how did it know the pattern of its next stage? How did it know to change its blueprint from the structure of peat to that of coal and eventually diamond?

The answer is that it absorbed the new patterns in two ways. First, from the actual experience of going through the changes. Second – and this is crucial – the carbon elemental was already harmonically connected to all the other carbon elementals in existence, including the greater carbon angels. Through this connection, the elemental was telepathically aware of the bigger picture. It could therefore flow into the relevant pattern for its next stage, because other devas had been through it all before.

To continue the life story, the young carbon elemental then came close to the roots of a plant. Its awareness now expanded to include the way in which a plant absorbs nutrients and moisture from the earth (plants and animals are essentially carbon-based organisms). Again, through the process of harmonic resonance, the little elemental absorbed the blueprint of how a root system works and also connected with the greater blueprint of this process throughout the plant kingdom.

In the language of the West, the carbon elemental of the earth had expanded to become a tiny gnome, aware of the root absorption process. In poetic language, we could call the angel who holds the blueprint for the whole process the Gnome King.

The elemental was drawn to a small plant. It then became an elf, the name given in English to devas of plants and bushes. If it had gone on to become associated with a flower, it would in the English tradition have been called a fairy.

Connected now with a single plant, it also connects harmonically with all the other similar elves and also with the greater angel who holds the picture for the plants as a whole. This greater angel could here be called an Elf King. If it were associated with flowers, we could call it the Fairy Queen.

One possible line of evolution for this little elf is to become especially connected with trees. It could then evolve, for example, into the spirit of a great oak and later into the spirit of a cluster of trees, and even later into the overlighting spirit of a forest. It could become a Pan.

Our elf, however, found itself looking after a shrub near a church and its awareness was gradually touched by the sound of organ music, the choir and the harmonic of the congregation's prayers. It was so stimulated by this experience that it began to expand its awareness to include the church and was gradually drawn into the energies that surround religious worship. In Western language, the word 'cherub' (plural 'cherubim') describes a deva who is helping these energies of prayer and praise.

So it was that the carbon elemental became a nature spirit and then evolved to become part of the deva community holding the pattern for perfect religious worship. This deva might just as easily have become involved in human affairs through gardening or being attracted to children playing.

This 'life story' shows that devas flow through different stages in their history and do not die in the same way as plants, animals and humans. They do not dramatically lose their bodies, but flow continuously through their stream of evolution. As they evolve, their consciousness expands and the patterns which they hold become ever larger and more complex.

Other Starting Points

But, as explained earlier, deva elementals do not simply exist in dense matter. They also exist in water, gas and fire. Devic essence holds together the emotional and mental energy fields, as well as the intuitive and spiritual levels. These elemental devas have paths of evolution connected not to nature but to human beings and the great fields of thought and emotion, or to the energies, rays and dimensions that move invisibly through the universe. The vast fields of space which seem to modern science to be a vacuum are in fact huge fields of energy with deva life permeating the total fabric of the universe.

Within the context of the human environment, many devas begin their evolution within the fields of emotion and thought. This means that their major source of experience is human life, in the same way as other devas are intimately connected with plants or animals.

A deva that begins as an emotional elemental may follow a line of evolution associated purely with human energy fields. Or it may follow a stream that goes beyond individual humans into the clouds of mood and emotion that float around the planet. Equally, a deva that begins as a thought elemental may go on to be associated with the great archetypes of thought, such as the ideas of justice or democracy. This will be discussed in Chapter 9.

A Self-aware Spirit

Incidentally, it is traditional in the West that devas are called 'angels' when they reach a level of self-consciousness about their own existence. This is very similar to the difference between animals and humans. When animals become aware of themselves as beings in their own right, we call them human. Devas also go through this stage of evolution. A logical definition of an angel, therefore, is a self-aware spirit.

Gravity and Decay

There are also some devas whose basic vibrations are not comfortable or healthy for us, as well as others which have been 'damaged' by their interaction with humanity. These will be looked at in Chapter 8, on healing.

Magnetic Attractors and Freedom of Expression

The beginning of this chapter described how devas tend to be passive. But this passivity holds great power—for the blueprint and energy pattern of the angel magnetically attract its companion to fulfilment. This magnetism is part of the natural flow of the universe. Although it appears passive in our dimension, it transmits cosmic power. So the deva's pattern is like a signpost which not only points the direction but encourages us and draws us into our future.

But although our fulfilment is in the future, the deva experiences it now. In a certain way, devas transcend time. And because of their harmonic telepathy with all other devas, they also transcend space. So while a careless gardener or bad weather may interfere with a plant, the nature spirit still holds the pattern of its perfect growth to guide the plant into its future.

This magnetic blueprint is inspiring, not controlling. The blueprint, the angel's energy field, is an open matrix within which lies the freedom of many choices. The proof of this freedom is the kaleidoscopic complexity of life. No single flower or person or work of art or relationship or ceremony is exactly like any other.

The spirit attracts its partner to fulfilment, but inside that fundamental attraction is space for diversity, change and creativity – for individual genius, eccentricity and limitations. The pattern is perfect, but anything can happen within it. You could, for example, be inspired by the same muse that accompanied Mozart, but the result would be different. You could also be inspired by the same muse that overlit Leonardo da Vinci, but your picture might hang by magnets on a fridge. You could be inspired by the same Cupid who inspired the great lover Don Juan, but ... ah well.

Devas impose no constraints on their more active and material companions. They simply hold the pattern and inspiration. This is what is 'angelic' about them. Call someone 'angelic' and you are saying that they harm no one but are gently inspiring. They attract us to fulfil ourselves.

The Archetypal Connections

The magnetic power of an angel is harmonically connected to all other similar angels. Thus all rose fairies, for example, are harmonically connected and carry the same basic pattern for the perfect rose. They are also all connected to a far larger rose spirit who holds the general pattern, the archetypal awareness, for all roses.

There is what we might call a Rose Angel, a very large and complex being which holds within its consciousness all rose bushes and rose devas across the planet. This is an old and classical idea. Plato, using different language, described these archetypal beings as 'perfect forms'. This older and more experienced deva holds in its awareness the experience of all the other rose spirits. The Rose Angel is an archetype holding the classical pattern for the whole family.

Similarly, the fairy of a rose flower is holding its awareness in two directions. First, it is holding its pattern and matrix over the individual flower. Second, it is fully open to its connection with the greater nature spirit who holds the pattern for all the flowers of that species. Its focus is earthed in its companion and at the same time open to the greater archetype.

It is because of this permanent connection with the archetypal Rose Angel that the individual fairy stays stable while its flower deals with all the changes imposed on it by the environment. This is why, whatever happens to the flower, the fairy maintains its open connection with the angel of the species and the archetypal pattern.

Within this framework you can see how spirits too learn from their experience and accumulate wisdom. The rose fairy magnetically registers all the factors that have affected its particular plant and does not forget them. This information is, in turn, telepathed to all the other rose devas and to the Rose Angel.

To understand why and how this works so well, you must be prepared to take a leap into mystic awareness or simple trust. This will tell you that nature and the universe are benevolent and powerful. There is a loving plan and purpose unfolding through all life, from an exploding star system to a single blade of grass. If you know or experience this to be true, the whole creative pattern of angel evolution makes perfect sense.

This is one reason why mystics so like the company of devas. The deva awareness is naturally open to the benevolent dynamic of the universe, whereas we humans usually have to work hard to achieve that state of surrendered and relaxed expansion.

The Mystic Dimension

We are surrounded and permeated by devic life. Whether we know it or not, devas weave the very fabric of our atoms and bodies. When people feel alone and alienated, if they could just plug into the devic life in their own bodies they would find extraordinary nurture and connections. When mystics celebrate the magic and joy of life, this is something that they feel running through their whole being. The mystic awareness of connection and love is not a mental idea, but a full experience.

The isolation of life as we know and see it is an illusion. The flower may seem to stand alone, as may you or I. But linked to all of us are spirits ultimately attuned to the expansion and growth of the universe. This is why a connection with angels has always been so useful to people on the religious path. To be attuned to them is to be attuned to the great cosmic flow, to the Tao, to Zen, to the cosmic Christ.

Most mystic traditions espouse the idea that God is the beginning and end of everything, transcending time. We, on the other hand, must pass through time and experience in order to grow. But devas are like that concept of deity, because they too already know the beginning and end of their fulfilment.

5

Sensing a Deva

A S A CHILD you may have told someone that you had sensed something unusual, seen some strange lights, heard a peculiar noise, only to receive the reply, 'Yes, of course, dear. But it's all in your imagination.' However loving and well-meant, this kind of parental response may have blocked you from making a relationship and learning from spirits who are really there.

Anyone who is reading this book will have experienced spirits but may not have known it. Western society and culture have not supported the registering, understanding and valuing of this kind of experience.

It is also true that experiencing spirits is subtle. It is not registered through the usual five senses and you will not have been taught how to notice and understand the experiences. Again, you have probably thought that all your experiences were pure imagination.

Time and time again in my classes I have had the pleasure of hearing people talk cautiously about their imagined experiences of devas. Then, as they discover that they are in a group of people who believe in them and understand them, they begin to grasp that what happened to them was real. We all experience a deep sense of relief and integration when we realise that other people have had similar experiences and similar doubts.

At the same time it is appropriate to add a supportive word about scepticism. In ordinary daily life we do not believe everything we see and hear: our natural scepticism and curiosity keep us asking questions. This is healthy. When we begin to sense the work with spirits, our scepticism and intelligence should stay alert. It is worth remembering that in folklore the people who commune with spirits are usually called wise women and men; they are not stupid, gullible people who believe anything.

So with that caution, let us look at how we actually do the sensing. How do we know anything is there? How do we know it's true? How do we know that we haven't made it all up? How do we discriminate?

How We Sense It All

The key to understanding all this is very straightforward. We have an energy field, as well as a dense physical body. We sense and feel things in our energy field. Devas and spirits, on the other hand, do not have dense physical bodies but they do have energy fields. So when spirits are in our energy field, we can feel them.

VIBRATIONS IN OUR ENERGY FIELD

By 'energy field' I mean a phenomenon as normal as the magnetosphere around the earth shown in atlases, or the electric field of the conger eel which is powerful enough to electrocute and kill large animals. This energy field radiates from and permeates our physical body. It is made up of what we in the West often call vitality and in Hinduism is called prana. It is also made up of more subtle energies and radiations associated with emotions, mind and spirit. All of this is part of the foundation of Ayurvedic (Indian), Chinese and holistic medicine. It is also often called the aura. It permeates our physical body and extends beyond it.

If a new or unusual or distinct energy comes into our field, we notice it because it sets up a new vibration or disturbance in our own field. This 'disturbance' vibrates through the aura into our physical body, which registers the sensation through the nerves and chemical changes. This is usually as subtle as a change in temperature or humidity. But sometimes the feeling is very clear.

To sense devas we have to give special attention to what we are sensing in our field. Although subtle, it is also visceral – of the flesh and blood. Something comes into your energy field. You feel it because it creates an impression on your physical body and nervous system – like hairs going up on the back of your neck or a distinct change of mood.

Spirit Sensations and the Third Eye

The real lesson, therefore, is learning how to notice and feel what is going on in our energy field. For most people this is a problem, because we are simply not in the habit of giving attention to what we feel in our auras.

However, here is some good news. Once you take the trouble to give it some attention, it is surprisingly easy. You just have to be more playful with your imagination. Some people, of course, are more sensitive than others, but I have never met anyone who is completely insensitive.

Let us look more closely now at the mechanics of perception.

THE MECHANICS OF PERCEPTION

The human aura experiences the new or different energy as a ripple of disturbance which comes down through it to the nervous system. The nervous system, in turn, transmits its message to the mind–brain. The mind–brain then has to notice and interpret it.

If the sensation is too subtle the mind–brain will ignore it, because other more important experiences or sensations are being received. Noise and movement round about, or internal sensations of excitement, anxiety and other normal moods, will block out more subtle sensations.

This is why people need to get into a contemplative mood to perceive devas. Most people's natural sensitivity is overlaid with layers of psychological armour and the habits of living in the modern world. If you need a few days to unwind on holiday before you can feel the good things of life again, you will know what is meant.

Intense activity – physical, emotional or mental – also increases the coarseness and shielding of our mind and nervous system, limiting our range of perceptions. When in a wound-up state we hardly notice the beauty of a sunset, or a child's smile, or a change in the direction of the wind – let alone the more subtle realities of the deva world.

In Chapter 3 I described what happened at the end of my six-month ceremony. When I knelt before the altar to make my final call to the angel, it seemed as if nothing was there. I was so anxious that I was blocking any awareness of what was going on at a more subtle level. It was only after relaxing that I could sense what was happening.

So you have to learn how to be quiet. It is not difficult, as will be explained later in this chapter. Once you are quiet, your mind–brain has to interpret the sensation and register it in a way that makes sense.

A few mind–brains translate the sensations into clear images, which is called clairvoyance. But the images are created by the mind. Many Westerners are desperate to *see* fairies and angels. But the 'seeing' is never real in the way we see things through our physical eyes. There is no impression through the retina, which is why blind people can be clairvoyant. The mind is clothing the sensation in familiar images. A clairvoyant of my acquaintance states very clearly that her clairvoyance is often a hindrance, and she always has to check whether the imagery in her mind is an accurate representation of the energy she is feeling.

Some people translate the sensation into words, which is called clairaudience. It is obvious, isn't it, that an English speaker 'hears' the spirits in English; a Portuguese hears them in Portuguese and so on. And a few people smell spirits.

However, the vast majority of people just sense and have a feeling of something being there. You may want to see pictures or hear noises because that is so much more obvious than a subtle sensation; but even if you do, the pictures and sounds still need interpreting and assessing. There is, incidentally, some evidence to suggest that the part of the physical brain which registers and interprets the sensations is towards the front behind the forehead. This, then, would be the fabled third eye.

Is the Perception Real and Accurate?

Unfortunately there is no easy solution to this business of accuracy. It is, of course, frustrating for most people that they cannot be sure whether an impression is real or just a projection of their imagination – this is why charlatans and deluded psychics get away with rubbish. Beware of anyone working with spirits who claims one hundred per cent certainty about their impressions. Beware of anyone working in this field who does not explain that there is always a margin of error or who is not humble about their work.

The trick is to go quiet and allow an impression to settle in your mind–imagination. It is impossible to get a clear impression if you are at all agitated. Also, any emotional excitement or neediness will affect the way that your mind–imagination interprets the impression. Many of us tend to exaggerate our experiences to compensate for an insecure ego, and this can starkly affect how we interpret sensations in our aura.

Equally, you cannot trust your impressions if you are over-serious or too earnest, which is another way of tensing your body and mind. Spirits are energy beings, and energy is always moving. Earnestness is the sign of an immobile attitude.

It is unwise to want a clear and simple truth. This kind of work is about sensing devas, not about adding numbers. It is more lyrical than mathematical. In Pythagoras's mystic school in ancient Greece there was a clear understanding of this paradoxical relationship between mathematical accuracy and poetic art. The harp must be tuned perfectly. But the music that resonates is harmonic and descanting, not rigid and bound by material logic.

This is also reflected in the waves of beauty that emerge out of modern chaos theory, which attempts to understand the apparently unpredictable behaviour of systems governed by external forces. There are fixed mathematical constants at the base of the equation, but they manifest and emerge chaotically. Yet out of the chaos emerge patterns of beauty.

A further requirement is a kind of positive scepticism. With all the psychological and cultural baggage that we carry, it is important to keep an open and self-reflective sceptical mind.

Because spirits are not the same as human beings, and because you are beginning to explore a new dimension of life, you must remember that you are a newcomer. The spirit reality has always been there, but you are now beginning something new. Some of it may feel familiar, but expect and be open to new sensations, some clear and obvious, some very subtle and ethereal.

If you follow how your energy field transmits a message into your nervous system, you will understand that your whole body is the sensor for registering spirits. So be relaxed and aware of your body.

Finally, your mind–imagination has a natural instinct to play with and interpret the sensations in your energy field. It is important to understand that the actual images, sounds or words are merely symbolic clothing on top of the actual experience. They are not the experience, but are suggestive of it.

The end result is not that you will be receiving clear and accurate messages like letters, telephone calls or e-mails. The deva realm is more like the weather or swimming in the ocean or sailing or music. It is a series of moods and atmospheres and sensations – and you begin to trust that they are real.

To summarise:

- Be calm. You cannot trust any impression if you are in an excited state.
- Have a relaxed attitude and a sense of humour. Take none of this seriously.
- Have an open and lyrical state of mind.
- Stay in a continuous state of self-assessment. This is a process and not a one-off product.
- Expect to experience new moods and atmospheres. Remember, this is a learning process.
- In order to sense what is in your field, you must be relaxed and aware of your body.
- Learn the art of allowing your mind–imagination to play with the sensation, with an awareness that it is not necessarily the reality.

Catch the Change in the Atmosphere

By now you will have appreciated that pictures or sounds are not important. The important things are the sensation and its quality – the changes in atmosphere.

You may want to see a fairy dressed in a tutu and with silver wings, but isn't it far more interesting to notice how the flower deva actually feels inside your aura? You may want to see a healing angel in the form of the Archangel Raphael, golden and with huge wings, but it is far more important that you catch its atmosphere within you. A conversation that has frequently taken place in my workshops will illustrate the point.

'I was in the forest,' a student will recount excitedly, 'and I saw flashing lights shimmering in the air. These are fairies, aren't they?'

'Maybe,' I reply. 'But what was the quality of atmosphere when you saw the lights?'

'They were mainly silver with some red and green flashes,' the student answers, staying fixed on the visuals.

'I understand that,' I persist, 'but what did they *feel* like?'

'What did they feel like?' Irritation is mounting.

'Yes.'

The student will often close her eyes in order to focus and remember.

'It was like a word we've all been using,' she answers. 'It was magical.'

'Can you remember how it felt in your energy field?' I ask. 'What did your body register?'

'It tingled. It was fun. And also a bit scary.'

'Scary?'

'Yes, because it was so new and different.'

'Would you like to have stayed with the sensation in order to explore it – even though it frightened you a bit?'

'Of course!'

As the student says 'Of course' I can almost see her mind lighting up. Typically, she has been so focussed on the lights that she has almost missed the real experience. She will also have been a little bit nervous because it was a new experience, which will have been another reason for not going more deeply into it.

Stretching the Tingle

Beginners commonly experience a sense of something magical that lasts only a few seconds – a light, a colour, a smell or a touch. This often happens in parks, gardens and woods. It also happens frequently in people's homes, during counselling and therapy sessions, in creative moments and randomly. For a second or so there is a tingle, a sense of magic in the air, a fleeting moment of something strange, haunting and attractive. Everything may shimmer into another reality. You may think you see sparkling lights in the air, or hear a tune floating in the ether. The trees or plants may seem to change colour.

Your attention is attracted to this new reality, but there is no blatantly obvious signal from the spirit world – no deva dressed in uniform greeting you. You want a more obvious signal, but you do not get it. So you let the experience pass. But your nervous system was indeed registering some deva presence and activity.

If you want to explore what is really happening, you need to pause, relax and monitor what else you are feeling. This is not difficult. Be still and receptive, and wait to see what you feel and sense.

The challenge is to take these magical moments and stretch them for longer than a few seconds. But do not expect any more flashing lights or tinkling sounds. Open the door of your inner perceptions. Go quiet and monitor the subtle impressions you sense.

Joanna was visiting some friends in a tower block on a desolate east London council estate. For a while she sat in the window of the fourth-floor flat looking down at the small patch of scruffy grass and the few straggly trees in between the buildings. The view seemed ugly, but the sun was out and the sky was blue. She began to relax, and suddenly she heard bells tinkling.

This noise was in her mind, and she took it as a signal that something was happening in her energy field. She relaxed more deeply and let herself begin to sense and feel the surroundings. She could feel the energies, and her mind–imagination immediately clothed them in archetypal images. In the middle of a depressed inner city area she sensed and saw elves and fairies dancing in procession on the grass, around the trees, and in and through the small children's playground.

In a normal, closed frame of mind she could not have imagined that the dancing life of nature spirits would exist in a place like that. But, relaxed in the sun, she could clearly sense it there. She had to choose, however, to be aware.

The One Important Skill

By now you will be well aware that there is one fundamental skill in sensing devas: the ability to be inwardly quiet and feel the mood or atmosphere around you. A lot of pompous hocus-pocus has been uttered about acquiring this skill – that it only comes with great powers of concentration, or is only granted to those who are spiritually pure. As far as I am concerned, however, if you can watch television or a film, or listen to music, or look at a landscape, for more than five minutes you possess the skill.

You just need to be able to keep quiet for a while in a relaxed way. There are thousands of books that teach relaxation, but in fact most people know what it is like to sit quietly and calmly. If you want some extra help buy one of the many relaxation tapes, including mine (see p. 163), that are available or experiment with several to see what works best for you.

Here is a technique for relaxation and centring that I find very helpful.

RELAX AND CENTRE

Sit or stand in any comfortable position. For two minutes do absolutely nothing. Gradually everything will begin to calm down. If after two minutes it is not, wait a while longer. If you are patient, sooner or later things will begin to slow down.

When you are ready, begin to turn your attention down

into your body. Your chest and your abdomen form a huge cave. In this cave are all your internal organs. Feel happy that they are there. Greet them. Hold your attention down into your body for a while.

Then take your awareness down into your lower stomach. Take a few comfortable breaths down into your lower stomach. If you feel like making a sighing sound or a noise of release, go ahead.

Be relaxed and comfortable in your body.

Notice the rhythm of your breath and how it feels as it flows in and out of your nostrils. Be gently aware of your body and the earth beneath you. Wait patiently. Unwind.

If your mind is too busy, do not be frustrated or judgemental about it. Just recognise that it is part of your busy life and give it some time to calm down. Have an understanding and friendly attitude to your mind.

Wait patiently.

The more times you do this, the easier it becomes.

In some tribal and shamanic traditions, the stillness is brought about by rhythmic drumming and dance. The pulse of the drum and the movement of the body seduce the personality into being quiet – sometimes called a trance-like state, but always conscious. Again, you can buy tapes of this music.

Making Your First Connections

Now to see how easy it is to put this into practice. It may help you to work with a friend, because afterwards you can discuss your impressions.

FIRST CONNECTIONS

First, place yourself in a situation where there are devas you want to meet, and where you feel comfortable. This will vary according to the kind of person you are and what you like doing. Here is a short list of possibilities that you might like to explore:

- In your home – spirit of the household.
- Next to a favourite plant – deva of the plant.
- In a church, temple, synagogue or other place of worship – angel of worship.
- Outside in beautiful landscape – landscape angel.
- If there is a park or church, or river or mountain, where you have always felt a presence, those are also good places to start.

Then, when you are ready, use the technique for getting quiet and centred that I have just described, or the one that works best for you. Remember that an attitude of patient acceptance is the key.

Remember that an excited body or personality will prevent you sensing the subtle presence. Equally, do not be too serious or earnest. Just be relaxed and philosophical. Sit there waiting with no expectations.

When you feel ready, but without changing your quiet mood, let your attention drift to scan and feel the air around you. Give very quiet attention to what you are sensing. Your mind may want to protest or question. Gently accept anything your mind does.

Then, in a style that suits your personality, with or without words, acknowledge the presence of the deva. *I know you are here. I recognise and acknowledge your presence.*

Stay relaxed, and notice any impression or feeling or sensation. Be very patient and notice what you feel and what passes through your mind.

Some people may receive an impression first time. Others will have to do it several times before trusting that they sense something. It may take several visits and contemplations before you feel that you are coming into a real rapport and relationship.

For some people the experience of the inner realm will be very obvious. For others it is very subtle. Be prepared to notice and believe in the insubstantial sensation and ethereal impression.

If you feel you have a mental block to this work, you might find it useful to make some affirmations. These can quickly and deeply transform lower mind patterns that are sabotaging what you want to do.

AFFIRMATIONS FOR WORKING WITH SPIRITS

Using the method that works best for you, bring yourself to a point of calm. Then aloud or silently begin to say one or more of the following affirmations. Alternatively, make up your own.

- I am sensitive and open to devas and angels.
- My mind does not block my sensitivity.
- The universe supports me in working with spirits.
- God loves me and God loves spirits. God loves us to work together.
- I work with devas to heal and transform the world.
- The world needs me to work with spirits.
- Working with spirits is part of my spiritual path.
- Being aware of spirits helps me grow and serve.

At first you will probably find it difficult to speak these affirmations as if they are true and authentic. But repeat them, as often and as regularly as you need to, until you feel them to be true.

Be realistic about the fact that you are just building up a relationship with the spirits. Familiarity only comes with time: if you want a relationship and an attuned awareness you must regularly spend time working at it. One of the greatest pleasures in your life will be coming back to places and situations where you are in relationship with its spirit. It is like coming back to an old friend.

Which Plane, What Vibration?

Before closing this chapter it is worth looking at the different energy fields in which spirits and angels have their focus. If you want to go a step further this information will help you fine-tune your sensitivity and perceptions. If not, just pass on to Chapter 6.

Human beings are simultaneously physical, emotional, mental and spiritual beings. But according to our mood we may be predominantly focussed at one level. One day your focus may be physical, on food and sex, but on another day you may be in a philosophical or contemplative mood and your focus is mainly mental.

Some devas are like us, simultaneously focussed at different levels, but others have specific energy fields in which they work. Nature spirits, for example, are bound to have much of their focus in the dimension of physical vitality or prana, the field of energy which vitalises all living creatures. A cherub of devotional religious ceremony may be principally focussed in the realm of emotion. An inspiring muse of architecture may be focussed only in the energy field of thought. Similarly a gnome is predominantly focussed in earth, a salamander in fire, a sylph in air and an undine in water.

So whenever someone tells me that they have had an experience of a spirit, I always ask two questions. What did it feel like? And in what energy field was the deva focussed?

To achieve greater accuracy of perception when working with spirits, the following meditation exercise has much to recommend it. It is based on the principle of the natural hierarchy of energy fields.

Earth is the densest energy field, followed by water and then air. Then we move into the dimensions of pure vitality, of prana and etheric energy (many people can see the etheric shimmer of a tree around its physical body). Beyond the etheric level are the fields where emotions exist, then the levels of mind and thought, and beyond them the planes of the soul, intuition and spirit. To help with this exercise, I have reproduced the diagram used in Alice Bailey's books.

Pure Spirit
Intuition
Light Thought
Medium Thought
Dense Thought
Light Emotion
Medium Emotion
Dense Emotion
Different Levels of Prana and Vitality
Air
Water
Earth

Your consciousness rises up the planes, becomes familiar with them and how they feel.

GOING UP THE PLANES

As always, bring yourself to centre in the way that is easiest for you. Make sure you are comfortable, for this exercise may take a little while. It is also, for some people, a very useful way to come into meditation.

When you feel calm and focussed, turn your attention to the material earth. Let your awareness go into earth and feel what it is like. Open your awareness to the different spirits which exist in earth. Notice any impressions or thoughts.

Now gently take your focus into the dimension of water and do the same procedure.

When you are ready, move on to air.

Then the field of energy directly closest to air (this would be the fourth).

Then those beyond it – the fifth, sixth and seventh.

Then let your awareness open to the emotional fields of energy – what they feel like and the spirits which exist in them. Try going up seven emotional planes, but if seven does not work use a method that suits you.

Then move into the mental-thought planes of energy.

And after that to the realms of intuitions and pure spirit.

At a certain point you will feel that you have gone far enough. Relax completely. And gently release the whole exercise.

After doing this exercise, your consciousness will probably be in a pleasant, meditative state. Stay there as long as you want.

If you ever feel over-excited by the exercise, stop doing it. Connect with the earth, hug a tree, and allow your body and brain to feel the soothing presence of soil and nature.

6

Attunement and Action

THIS CHAPTER EXPLAINS how easy the next step is, which is to come into a relationship of cooperation with devas. Such a relationship is supportive and healing in so many ways.

Activity, 'Actor' and Spirit

While I was teaching the early workshops at Findhorn I discovered a simple three-part format that underlies all cooperation with spirits: the activity, the 'actor' and the spirit of the activity. So, for example, you might have:

Actor	Activity	Spirit
Artist	Painting	Muse
Healer	Healing	Healing angel
Gardener	Pruning	Fairy
Business person	Business	Mercury (spirit of good communication)

You contemplate and attune to the activity and the spirit of the activity. Then you act.

Why should you want to do this in the first place? The spirit of the activity, the deva, holds in its energy field the pattern for the perfect fulfilment of that activity. So, as you open your awareness to sense the deva, you yourself become enveloped and connected by the deva's awareness. The deva's blueprint of perfect fulfilment is now connected with your own field. This guides, inspires, colours, re-vibrates and tones what you are doing and how you do it.

What follows is a more tabular illustration of this relationship between actor, activity and spirit.

Gardener attunes to	Rose bush	
	Rose bush deva – *Rose fairy* (Inner pattern of perfect bush)	Then gardener acts
Healer attunes to	Ill person	
	Healing angel – *Raphael* (Inner pattern of perfect healing)	Then healer acts
Worker attunes to	Business	
	Angel of business – *Mercury* (Inner pattern of perfect business)	Then worker acts
Lover attunes to	Relationship	
	Angel of relationship – *Cupid/Eros* (Inner pattern of perfect relationship)	Then lover acts
Human attunes to	Personal growth	
	Angel of personal growth – *Guardian Angel* (Inner pattern of perfect growth)	Then human acts

In Chapter 2 I described how certain South Sea islanders build their ocean-going canoes using ritual at each stage of construction. Songs and ceremonies are their method for attuning to the boat and the spirits of the perfect vessel.

Boat builder attunes to   Boat

                               Boat spirit
                               (Inner pattern
                               of perfect boat)   Boat builder acts

And as the boat builders progressed with their work they attuned to other friendly spirits. In the first stages they attune to the spirit of the forest and the trees to help select the right trunk. Whilst carving the trunk, they may also attune to Neptune and the sprites of the ocean, to have true inspiration for carving the smooth lines that will cut the water.

It Really Is Easy and Natural

At first, the idea of inviting in the spirits may seem difficult or unusual – in fact it is easy and nothing out of the ordinary. You just need to be open to feeling and sensing the inner beauty and creativity of life. I have never met anyone who has not at some time been touched by the magic of landscape, or rippling water, or dancing fire, or music, or art, or a smile.

It requires only a small use of your imagination. Chapter 5 explained how straightforward it is to notice and sense the presence of devas. In this next step, let the impression touch your mind–brain and then watch how your mind–imagination interprets it.

What you are doing now is deliberately inviting into your field a particular spirit. They have no resistance and flow like water down a hill into this relationship. It is their purpose to be in rapport with us, no matter how wayward we may be. In *The Deva Handbook* Nathaniel Altman writes:

It wasn't that the devas were not interested in communicating with me, but rather that I had blocked myself from reaching out to them .... I had adhered to the widespread belief that I was both separate and autonomous from nature, and I had tended to see the non-animal world as one made up of objects – not as a world of living beings to whom I was intimately connected.

Thought Creates Vibration

Devas are called in using a form of telepathic vibration. Just thinking of them creates the vibration. The vibration from the thought makes a harmonic connection and attracts their attention and they turn towards you. Their response follows a basic law of physics: like attracts like. Thinking of a particular deva creates an electromagnetic signal which ripples out holographically – it is felt through space and the inner dimensions in a way that is not obstructed by time or distance. This basic principle is accepted by all mystic, occult and shamanic traditions.

So to invite spirits in, you need to have some idea of them in the first place. But this idea does not need to be a full and intimately familiar technicolour vision – the slightest idea of them works. Simplicity and purity of intention are all that is really needed.

Some people worry because they do not even have a general idea of a spirit. 'How can I think of it or call it in when I don't know anything about it? I've never worked with spirits before. I'm a complete beginner.' A couple of examples will help you solve this difficulty. Suppose you want to call in an angel of your home. Stop for a moment and imagine what that spirit would be like. At its most basic *it will be some kind of energy or atmosphere that floats in or around your home, and its presence will bring some kind of blessing to your home.* That last sentence is all the awareness you need to make the connection in the first place.

PREPARATORY WORK

If you are about to engage in some activity and you want to call in deva cooperation, first spend a while thinking about what you are about to do and what you want. Do it several times until you feel that you have a good grasp of the issue. What are the problems and challenges? What kind of outcome do you want? What kind of style do you want? What materials are you using? Is there anything special about the environment? And so on. It would be stupid, for example, to prune a bush for the first time in your life without previously reading or obtaining some practical, experienced advice.

Then just open your mind and your heart to the possibility that there is a spirit who understands the issue perfectly and knows how to help. This deva absolutely understands the style and form needed, and all the challenges and possibilities. This deva already has a real sense of how it can be perfectly completed. The spirit's awareness and energy field will bring an inspiring blessing.

Happily accept that such a spirit exists and that this spirit will flow easily into cooperating with you.

Invite and Acknowledge

The next stage is to issue an invitation and, telepathically or out loud, ask the spirit to be with you. The invitation is based on the contemplation you have already done. You have been attuning to and thinking of the spirit. The thought attracted it in the first place.

The telepathed or spoken invitation creates an opening in your energy field, like a vacuum, which draws the spirit in closer. It is also a more direct reaching out from you to connect with it.

The invitation should immediately be followed by a grateful acknowledgement of its presence.

THE BASIC INVITATION

Using the method that works best for you, bring yourself to a point of quiet centre.

Then, when you are ready, begin to contemplate the spirit. Open your mind and your heart to it.

Aloud or in silence, clearly issue your invitation in words

that feel authentic to you. Stay in quiet contemplation. Whether you actually sense something or not, accept that the spirit is with you. Silently or out loud thank it for being present.

Stay quiet and just notice any impressions, feelings or thoughts.

Before ending, give thanks again.

Here is the simple procedure for calling in a spirit for your home:

CALLING IN A HOUSEHOLD ANGEL

As always, relax and come to centre in the way that works best for you.

Calmly contemplate your home, letting your mind wander, for example, around the rooms and the other people who live in it. Then contemplate the angel who could be in your home, its presence bringing a blessing and helping you all to live together in a more harmonious, creative and healing way.

Then, aloud or in your mind, communicate words like: 'Angel of the home, I invite you to be here. Angel of the home, I thank you for your presence.'

Feel totally free to use whatever words work for you. Or you may not want to use words at all. You might prefer simply to light a candle and feel yourself inviting in and welcoming the spirit's presence.

It is important that you acknowledge its presence and thank it. Even if you are not certain that it is with you, act as if it is. It will surely be with you, even if you cannot in those moments sense it. Say or telepath words like: 'Angel of the home, I acknowledge and give thanks for your presence.'

Do not let your intellect get caught up with thoughts such as: 'I don't really know what this deva is like .... This is just my imagination playing tricks .... How can I tell if this is really here? ... I feel like such an idiot.' Suspend your normal mental disbelief and enter into a more playful and imaginative, more poetic and lyrical dimension.

Trust that your invitation and your grateful acknowledgement of its presence will work. Simply accept that the deva is
already with you.

Do not worry if you are uncertain about what is really happening.
After doing this kind of work for a while, you will find it much
easier to accept the subtleties. The sense of connection does not
come like a telephone call or letter. Sooner or later you will catch
a change of mood and atmosphere.

Remember, the sequence for all spirit relationships is:

- *Attune.* You attune to the activity and to the spirit of the
  activity.
- *Invite.* You invite the spirit in so that you can cooperate with
  it.
- *Contemplate.* You contemplate the impressions and inspira-
  tions you receive from the spirit's presence.
- *Act.* You do something that follows on from the impression
  and inspiration.

Gratitude and Communion

'Fairies! Attention! Quick march!' is not a constructive way to
call in landscape spirits to help you dig the garden. This aggressive approach is, of course, rude and nasty. But that is not the real
reason why it is not appropriate.

The reason why we communicate with spirits in a style that is
courteous and grateful is because that style puts us more easily in
resonance with them. Courtesy and gratitude are moods. They
create a vibration which harmonises with devas. To connect
more easily with devas, it helps if we are more like them.

Just by being quiet and contemplative for a few minutes we can
calm down a lot of our typical human spikiness and enter a more
harmonic and beautiful rhythm. Our breath and the pulse of life
within us become more graceful. In that mood, you may sense
devas as friendly companions. They are with you wherever you
are going, whatever you are doing.

Sensing devas is not like watching a football match or a stage musical, where there is a distance between you and the activity. You actually move into a sense of family or community with them. This is why people who work with spirits often say that they do not communicate with spirits, they commune with them. The ongoing sense of companionship and communion is one of the great joys of this work. Many people who work and live in isolation, particularly in the landscape or in holy places, have felt no loneliness or need for human company. The companionship of spirits was more than enough.

CONNECT AS YOU REALLY ARE

But although we connect easily with devas in the harmony of silence, being quiet is by no means the only time when we connect with them easily. We do so also when we are in a real flow or creative groove, when there is a beautiful rhythm and pulse. This can happen in many of our daily human activities.

You must at some time have experienced doing something and really enjoying the feel of it. Your actions and your attitudes had a satisfying hum to them. This can happen while you are cleaning the house, out running, doing business, making love ... at almost any time. The activity takes on a different timbre and quality, and becomes imbued with beauty and harmony.

It is one of the most wonderful experiences to be in the flow of some activity, and simultaneously to feel the companionship of a spirit. Have you ever sat by a tree or stream and felt its friendship? Imagine an invisible but very friendly tree at your side while you do the housework or finish the accounts or go for a walk.

This magic of angelic cooperation may come in very slow and careful activities or in a flow of frenzied creativity. Again, nearly everyone has experienced the exhilaration of catching a fabulous wave of fast creative energy. This is often described as the artist being inspired by the fire of his or her muse.

To the eye of someone who likes calm and reflective moods, it might seem impossible for this angelic connection to be made in the midst of staccato frenzy. But who would deny that Van Gogh or Beethoven were inspired by the highest of art's muses? There are wild dances and crazy drumming which are as much inspired by and connected to spirits as the more gentle practices. Like everything else in our universe, volcanoes have their great spirits. Human activity is sometimes volcanic – and healthy for it.

The point of all this is that you should not get sanctimonious about the subject of spirits. Cooperating with them is a practical daily business, and this connection can manifest in a way that suits your own character and the specific activity. A strait-jacketed attitude of spiritual self-control is wrong. You will need the discipline of pausing and contemplating. You will need trust to take you through the first gateway of experience. But beyond that, you need the freedom to be who you really are, warts and all, introvert or extrovert, wild dancer or quiet mouse.

Clearer Impressions

There are basically two ways in which you will receive impressions of how to behave and act. The first is that in your quiet contemplation you will catch a clear sense of what is needed next. Alternatively, you will not get clarity in the contemplative mood but will later have a clear instinct about what to do.

If you are to get clarity while you are contemplating, the key is to stay relaxed and patient. If you are stressed or impatient, all you will sense is the 'noise' of your mood. You can also help the process by looking at the situation from different angles and by being very open to new perspectives.

CLARIFYING YOUR IMPRESSIONS

In the style that best suits you, come to centre and attune both to the activity on which you are about to embark and to the spirit of the activity. In your own authentic style call in the spirit and gratefully acknowledge its presence.

Whether you can sense it or not, the spirit is now connected to your energy field. Stay very relaxed and calm. Allow yourself to feel some sense of goodwill and companionship with the spirit.

Now sit quietly for a while and be patient. Let your awareness begin to think of, or picture, the activity you are about to do. (Do not be concerned if you have difficulty getting clear images. This is not important.) Stay relaxed and imagine yourself doing the activity. What impressions do you catch? In particular, keep your eyes and forehead relaxed. Without any expectation, be receptive and open to any new ideas or feelings. Be very patient.

You may or may not get clear thoughts and images about what you are going to do. But you will probably pick up a feeling about the atmosphere and style in which to do the work. For example, if you are about to repair a car or clean a room, you may sense that it would be best to whistle cheerfully while doing the job. On the other hand, you might feel that you need to be more focussed and careful.

In the contemplation let your imagination play with new possibilities. This may include a new mood or a new attitude. Perhaps, to catch the essence of the activity, you need to be more mellow – or more intense, or more creative. Try to discard old and fixed ideas so that you are open to new concepts. The more relaxed you can be about letting your imagination play, the more scope there is for inspiration.

If you stay long enough in this contemplative process, you may pick up a whole scenario for what you should do. And you can, of course, repeat the attunement and call several times until you feel confident about moving ahead.

You may not get immediate clarity, but if you do this exercise several times and you give yourself time to contemplate the activity, new ideas and inspiration will definitely come to you. Sven, the Scandinavian businessman in Chapter 2 who attuned to the angel of his factory, did not act overnight. He went into the factory early every morning, called in the angel, and then contemplated and noted the impressions passing through his mind. It was only after a while that he felt confident about what needed to be done, and then he acted.

CHECKING RELIABILITY

From within your contemplation you can begin to scan whether your impressions are reliable. Only do this when you have already clearly picked up a sense of what to do. If you switch on your scepticism too soon, you can sabotage and block the whole process.

Always staying calm and relaxed, you need to ask very ordinary and grounded questions of the following kind. Does this feel wise? Will it hurt anyone or anything? Is it an improvement on what I was already doing? Does it serve my maturing process and growth? What are the implications? Does it serve the situation? Do I have a sense that it is all right to go ahead?'

When you go through this process be wise about the kind of personality you are. If you tend to be over-critical or too cautious, these traits will colour your reflection on these questions. Conversely, if you are impulsive you will have other tendencies.

And if your mind starts to moan about not getting the kind of crystal clarity you want, remind yourself that life is always a learning process.

Following the Blue Light

If you do not get clarity in your contemplation, you may be concerned – even overwhelmeed with doubts. But it will help if you remember how often people work unconsciously with devas. For example, huge numbers of artists and musicians are unaware of their spirit companions. Concerts are filled with music angels, inspiring both musicians and audience. Jerry Garcia of the rock and roll band The Grateful Dead once said that their music worked because 'it kept following that blue light'. Clairvoyant friends of mind at their concerts had already noticed wonderful music spirits drawing the band's performance into the fulfilment of their genius. These muses are often experienced as very large clouds of colour and light, which are mirrored in the wonderful light shows that often accompany pop concerts. Other clairvoyants have noticed these music angels at tribal gatherings and classical concerts. These ideas are described in Cyril Scott's book *Music: Its Secret Influence*.

But it is not just artists who unknowingly have these invisible colleagues. Householders, business people, healers, therapists, gardeners, lawyers and many others also have their devas. They are accompanied by spirits who help them do their work in the best possible way. I would go so far as to assert that in general people who express either goodwill and kindness, or else creativity and genius, in their activities are accompanied by helpful spirits. You can recognise when you have this contact: you will tend to feel that your work is flowing, and you look forward to getting on with it.

In fact, looking forward with pleasant anticipation to an activity is a good indication that there may be a spirit connected with it. Your attitude will anyway tend to draw in an interested deva. Conversely, it is almost certain that if you do not look forward to cleaning your home, even if you have the time and energy, you are not connected to a household angel.

But all of this is unconscious for the vast majority of people. So if you are feeling uncertain about what to do next, take in the fact that you are not alone.

Put in practical terms, after you have attuned and called the spirit in, it does not really matter if you do not have a clear impression of what to do next – you were going to do the activity anyway. So look forward to it, get on with it and do your best. Follow the blue light. The performing musician cannot wait for clarity, because the audience and the rest of the band has its own timetable. The kitchen equally has to be cleaned.

When we have a spirit in our energy field, we can respond to that relationship instinctively. Like in sailing, as the wind and current change direction you adjust sails and angle and rudder. This cannot be expressed logically in the moment, but is a creative act of adjustment and intention. When a child on a bicycle begins to negotiate corners, you cannot say 'Lean ten degrees from the vertical.' There is a creative act happening here which is different for every corner and speed.

So it is when working with spirits. It is partly instinctive. Too much consciousness can make for wooden behaviour. You may want greater clarity and certainty, but this is not a logical set of dynamics. We are dealing here with instinct, intuition and possibilities. It is as much art as anything else.

But, you may insist, what about the deva's blueprint of how the activity can be perfectly fulfilled? Surely this is crystal-clear? No, it is not. The deva's blueprint is only a general idea about how the possibilities can be perfectly fulfilled.

There are a million different ways in which a tree can reach its full growth. However some of its mechanics such as cellular division and the need for moisture and light, cannot be changed. Equally, a classical violinist is stuck with vibrating the instrument's strings and staying within a score, but beyond that are matters such as the genius and timing.

So stay open to the feedback of self-reflection. Observe what happens. Learn lessons and know that you can do it better next time. You can only really tell whether the impression works and is useful as you put it into practice and reflect upon its value.

The Need to Act

A story told about a new gardener at the Findhorn Foundation, the Scottish community which has an interest in nature spirits, illustrates the problem of the avoidance of action. He was frequently found lying on the lawn when he ought to have been mowing it. When finally asked what he was doing, he replied that it was cruel to cut grass. He was therefore, he said, attuning to the grass and the grass spirits, and talking to them, suggesting that they should grow sideways to avoid their cruel fate.

He was moved on to another job.

Some people are naturally cautious, and working with spirits can make them so cautious that they would rather do nothing. They are worried that the impressions they receive are false and perhaps even harmful. As a result they become very reluctant to act.

The deva holds the inner pattern, but it requires human action in order for it to happen. A great painting is not created simply because the muse, the inspiration, is floating around. The painting is created because Leonardo puts brush to canvas.

Being attuned to the spirit world means that you have a wider and deeper perspective on life. It gives you greater freedom and greater presence. But always you have to act. The healer needs to move energy. The ritualist needs to move and speak symbolically. The gardener needs to dig or cut or plant. The business person needs to implement strategy. The artist needs to put pen to paper, finger to keyboard, chisel to stone. The spiritual path of working with devas is perfectly balanced. It is the human role to act.

7

Working More Closely
with Spirits

THIS CHAPTER WILL help you work more closely with our invisible companions. How far you take this work will, of course, depend on your individual circumstances. At one end of the spectrum is the occasional attunement; at the other end is holding open your awareness to the angel reality all the time.

The Human Environment

Your life is deeply and personally interwoven with devas whether you are aware of it or not. There is devic life all the way through your body, in every atom and organ, as well as in your emotions and mental energy.

We are particularly involved with spirits because on this planet we are great movers and shakers. Our effect on the physical world is substantial. In the energy fields of emotion and thought, however, we are the major influence and force. Our psyches, imagination, moods and thoughts are continually generating new currents and forms in the emotion–mind dimensions.

When you have a feeling or a thought, have you ever considered the energy that goes into it? When you express an emotion, emotional energy is moving. When you are thinking about something, you are also radiating thought energy. There are six billion people on the planet, all doing this.

Imagine what this looks like clairvoyantly from far away. The emotion–mind field must look like a great swirling, ever-changing ocean of complex currents and whirlpools and explosions. Each of us is involved in creating this. And this great moving field of energy affects each of us. In our own way, we are like water and wind and flames. We never stop moving, feeling and thinking.

To get a firm grasp on the angel realms it is important to understand and sense the reality of these inner dimensions of emotion and thought. The following exercise will be helpful.

THOUGHTFORM SPIRITS

Go silent and calm in the way that works best for you. Sit patiently for a little while and enjoy the stillness.

Then let you awareness begin to expand and reach out beyond where you are sitting. Be aware of how much space there is around you and around the earth.

When you have a sense of this space, give attention to the idea that it is filled with emotion and thought. Contemplate these huge fields of energy and begin to recognise that there are specialist clouds of emotion and thought floating around.

There are thoughtforms belonging to particular religions, for example. There are thoughtforms associated with film stars or political movements. Just let your awareness bob along contemplating these realities.

Recognise that these clouds have deva essence within them and that these clouds also have accompanying spirits.

Turn your attention now towards actually having a beautiful thought. Think something like 'I love nature' or 'I wish great success to someone.' Notice that just thinking and feeling this thought creates a movement of energy.

Contemplate that the energy of the thought contains devic essence.

Contemplate that your thought continues to float around, joining up with similar thoughts.

Contemplate that this cloud of thought, this thoughtform, has a deva looking after it, like a fairy looks after a flower.

Spend a while contemplating how many thoughtforms there are floating around. See which ones attract your attention. Notice that they have companion spirits.

Doing this exercise will help you appreciate how energetically important humanity is to the deva world. You are probably familiar with the sadness and protests expressed at the loss our forests, because of the beauty and complexity of these environments. These regions have also been the homes and communities of evolution for huge numbers of nature spirits. There are also huge numbers of spirits whose community of evolution is the human world of emotion and thought. Although some green activists might disagree, humanity too would be sorely missed. We are an important community for spirits on this planet.

Putting Energy into the Relationship

We humans wield huge amounts of energy in emotion and thought. We are not only fascinating as physical creatures, like tigers or whales, we are also fascinating as beings of psyche. When, in full consciousness, we reach out to the spirit world and seek to cooperate and commune, it is a significant and important action. Within you, you have elements that are mineral and plant and animal. You can be unconscious and lacking in awareness. But if you switch on your awareness and reach out to the angels, this is a significant event for them as much as it is for you.

Angels were described earlier as being passive in relation to the processes of nature. They hold the blueprint whilst we do all the activity. But in terms of the human–angel relationship, it is we who are passive! They are always there, aware of us, holding their maps to help us. We are not aware of them. We put very little into the relationship. There is even a huge section of human culture that dismisses their reality as fake imagination.

So when we actually bother to talk to them, we are creating important bridges between the life streams. Take this idea seriously and let it motivate you.

It is, however, crucial to realise that reaching out to make a relationship is not a day-dream. Some energy has to go into the relationship. This has always been a problem for romantic mystical types who prefer to stay in the realm of the imagination and avoid the physical world.

Some grounded activity is necessary: it can be physical, emotion or mental. There is a big difference between passive daydreaming and actually moving energy. When energy is moved, the real relationship begins and there is a genuine link between the worlds. I think that it is because of this bridging that many of us who work with angels have felt a sense of appreciation and gratitude from them.

It seems to me that spirits do not believe that we are genuinely reaching out to cooperate with them until they see some actual action from us. To feel that we are in relationship with them, they need us to put out some energy and do something. Let's look at this in some exercises.

DOING SOMETHING

Go quiet and calm in your own way.

Bring into your awareness any deva with whom you feel a connection. Spend a while just contemplating this spirit.

Notice how this could just be a day-dream.

Now begin to think of this deva with active thoughts of love. Telepathically send warm feelings to the deva.

Now return to your passive, contemplative state.

Notice the difference between contemplation and actively moving some energy.

Contemplate how your relationship with the spirit feels, now that you have put out some active energy.

This is similar to the exercise above, but instead of sending love do something else.

Go calm and bring a deva into your awareness. Here is an example. Telepathically attract the deva's attention by saying, 'Watch this.'

Then put some focussed mental energy into visualising

96

something like a sparkling golden star. Imagine that this star is filled with some of your energy and is now floating there, a form in its own right.

Then telepath directly to the spirit something like this: 'Look. I have created this star as a gesture of connection with you. I really know you are there. I am not day-dreaming. I value this connection.'

Relax completely. Go quiet, passive and contemplative. See what response you feel. Be open to any impressions.

Gently bring the exercise to an end. Give thanks.

The Invitation to Connect

The importance of actually doing something that moves energy can be very relevant when you are inviting a spirit into your life.

Chapter 6 explained that a proper invitation had to be communicated in order to make an authentic connection with the spirit. Whether you are calling in a home angel or a muse or nature spirit, you have to attune and issue the invitation. There are several different ways of doing this that are used across the world:

- Lighting a flame.
- Making an offering.
- Making a symbolic gesture.
- Making a sound.
- Speaking or telepathing the invitation in words.

Experiment to discover which style works best for you and for the spirits with whom you want to work. The exercise that follows will help you clarify this.

WHAT KIND OF INVITATION?

Go into silence and calm in the way that works best for you.

When you are pleasantly calm, gently contemplate the idea that you want to invite spirits to connect with you.

Then, when you are ready, begin to imagine and contemplate yourself lighting a candle to make the invitation. How does it feel to you in your contemplation? What are your impressions?

When you are ready, let your awareness move on and begin to imagine and contemplate yourself making an offering to spirits. Again, how does it feel to you in your contemplation? What are your impressions?

If you were to make an offering to it what would be appropriate? In many cultures some kind of grain or food is given. In others, flowers, crystals or money are given.

Notice whether you feel you need to create a space on which you can place the offering. Perhaps you want to create some kind of altar. Let the different possibilities pass through your mind. You can back this up with some research on altars and creating sacred space.

When you are ready, repeat the same procedure for making a symbolic gesture.

There are certain hand movements and body postures that often seem appropriate for connecting with spirits. The best known is that of going down on your knees and bowing to the earth. In other traditions, people may lift their arms up as if appealing to the sky or hold their hands out cupped as if to receive something. Most religious traditions have certain sacred symbols which their priests paint in the air with their hands or staffs. Other traditions use dance and sacred movement such as Yoga and Tai Chi.

Notice whether there is any instinctive feeling within you to work a certain posture or movement. Can you see yourself comfortably using certain body language and gestures? Does this style work for you?

Then move on again to look at making some kind of sound. In many cultures a noise is used to connect with spirits. This can be a song or a long tone. It can be rattling or drumming. It can be a sacred chant or hymn. It can be the deep resonant vibration of a didgeridoo or a long Tibetan trumpet. It can be a bell or cymbal.

Does this style feel good to you? Notice your impressions.

Then go through the process again for speaking or clearly telepathing the invitation.

You can do each part all in one long exercise or you look at them separately at different times. When you have contemplated all the styles, notice whether there is one with which you feel more comfortable.

Perhaps you will feel like experimenting with the different forms.

LIGHTING A FLAME

Take yourself into calm awareness and focus on the deva with whom you wish to work. Slowly and with awareness light a candle to honour it. Communicate in your own way that you are lighting the candle to honour it, issue your invitation.

Contemplate how this feels. Notice any impressions.

MAKING AN OFFERING

Have ready what it is that you are going to offer. Perhaps you will also have created some kind of altar.

Then go into your silence and, when calm, attune to the spirit whom you are inviting. Let your awareness connect with this spirit. Then, in your own style, greet it and tell it that you are making this offering to it.

Stay calm and very centred. Make the offering.

If you are out in the landscape, it may feel appropriate just to scatter or throw your gift.

Pause and contemplate the response of the spirit. Notice your impressions.

MAKING A SYMBOLIC GESTURE

Go calm and begin to contemplate the spirit with whom you want to cooperate. When you are ready, go into the movement or gesture that you feel will work. Stay calm and watchful as you do it. Communicate to the spirit that you are making this movement to honour it.

Then relax and contemplate how it feels to you.

MAKING A SOUND

Go calm and turn your attention towards the spirit. Staying calm, begin to make the noise and communicate to the spirit that this is being done to honour it. When the timing feels right, end the sound. Stay calm and contemplate how it all feels to you now.

In all of these exercises one of your most important guidelines will be what feels authentic for you. Work with what suits you and feels real. If in doubt, go for simplicity.

The Dance of Inspiration

The proof of a real relationship with devas is shown by acting in a way that is affected and influenced by the relationship. If the relationship has no effect on you, it is meaningless. But the inspiration to behave differently is not necessarily a logical process. Its outcome does not necessarily have to be wisdom – it may simply be playful.

When walking in a forest or landscape many people experience nature spirits. They see a flash of light, hear a strange sound, or suddenly feel something strange and magical. Having felt the connection, they may have an instinct to do something more than just walking or sitting. They may want to throw a stone into water, or kiss a tree, or do an unexpected little hop or spin or dance. Most people resist acting in this way, either not taking it seriously or afraid of appearing childish. But you should go ahead and do whatever is playfully moving through you. These acts reflect the harmonics of the nature spirits and deepen the connection.

PLAYING IN THE WOOD

Go into a piece of landscape which you love and come to a calm centre.

Greet the spirits of the landscape and open your energy field to connecting more closely with them. If it feels appropriate, give them some offering or do something else to signal your willingness to connect.

Stay very calm and centred and contemplate how the spirits feel in your energy field. Imagine how you feel in their energy field.

Let your mind–imagination be very playful in how it senses and interprets their energy. If you were to do something completely spontaneous, what would it be?

If you have an intuition or an instinct to do something, go ahead and do it.

Stay calm and centred, but do the action.

After the action, come back to being physically still. How does everything feel now?

When you are ready, give thanks.

This freedom to dance or spin or throw pebbles in response to the landscape devas is very similar to the artistic inspiration that can come from a muse. You cannot receive the full inspiration if you are wooden and over-serious. You must be prepared to let the life force flow through you in new ways.

CALLING IN A MUSE

Go calm in the way that works best for you, and then contemplate the work that you are about to do. Consider the outcome of the work itself, and the time and energy you are going to put in.

Begin to imagine a being who has a perfect sense of this whole creative process and who knows exactly how best to help you.

Make some gesture of connection with this being, this muse, and gratefully acknowledge her presence. Ask for her help and her ongoing presence while you are working.

Now stay quiet for a while longer. Do you have any suggestive images or thoughts? Particularly *sense* whether you are being inspired to work in a new mood or with a different attitude.

Thank the muse again.

Come gently out of the attunement and begin your work.

In an exercise like this you may find yourself being asked to behave in a way that is out of character for you, and difficult and challenging. You may find yourself being asked to change your emotional style or to ditch certain preconceptions.

Do not sabotage your freedom to move into something new because you are stuck in old patterns, or by rationalising that it is all over-imaginative. How you actually act in the end is your decision, but remember that you had the instinct for change and something new in the first place.

Creativity means that things are created anew and in new ways. This can be sudden and dramatic or slow and long-term. Consider the sudden kiss, the single brushstroke, the addition of extra pepper, the healing word and touch. At the other end of the scale think of the length and depth of constructing a cathedral or city, building your own life, or creating a deep and faithful relationship.

Margaret, a novelist, was once working to a very tight deadline when she started to experience writer's block and could not work out what should happen next in her story. So she did the exercise described above and deliberately called in a muse to unblock her. She went quiet and imagined its presence, and the clarity that it would give her about the plot and storyline. She called it in for creative direction.

In the contemplative silence during the connection, to her surprise and consternation she sensed a totally clear message.

The angel gave her no help at all with the actual book, but told her to take deep breaths regularly into the very lowest part of her stomach. She was disappointed with the advice but nevertheless followed it.

To help her remember she set her electronic watch to bleep every hour. She breathed deep into her belly and began to write. The block was gone. Every hour throughout the rest of the writing process the watch alarm would buzz and she would take a deep breath. She had no trouble writing her book after that.

It was not the kind of advice she was looking for, but it was crucial in helping her.

Earth, Water, Air and Fire

Many religious and tribal traditions recognise the important elements. Often they are placed at the four quarters of an equal-armed cross or a circle marking the four directions. Many songs and chants address this reality. One for example, runs:

> Earth my body,
> Water my blood,
> Air my breath,
> And Fire my spirit!

Associated with each of these elements are its elementals. Some mystic traditions make a specific point of attuning to these elementals, and in some initiation rites the candidate is not able to join the group fully until he or she has first been introduced to them.

The following exercise includes some paraphernalia and props, but please treat it very casually and with no pomp. The props are:

- For earth, a bowl of earth or salt or sand; or a crystal or rock. When you attune to the earth elementals you will be holding in your hand something representing earth, which helps to make the connection.
- For water, a jug of water and a glass. Pour the water to get the resonance of moving water.
- For air, a fan or feather which you move through the air in front of you. Alternatively, use incense: its rising smoke is emblematic of air.
- For fire, a candle or oil lamp which you light.

If you do not feel comfortable working with all the paraphernalia, do the connecting in silent attunement.

EARTH, WATER, AIR AND FIRE

First get everything together. Then find a quiet space and arrange yourself and your objects so that you are comfortable.

If you have family, ask them to leave you alone for twenty minutes – though many children love this kind of work. My feeling is that you should be relaxed enough that if a child wanders in you can greet him affectionately and be patient about guiding him on his way.

When you feel ready, use the method that works best for you to go into silence. Go calm and notice how comfortable your body feels. You are relaxed and centred. Spend a little while contemplating what you are about to do.

Acknowledge clearly that you are doing this for your education and to become more attuned to your environment.

Earth When you feel ready, pick up the representative of earth – the rock, crystal, soil, salt or sand. Hold it in your hand and contemplate how it feels. Extend your awareness to the elementals of earth. Greet them affectionately and invite them to be closer to you. You may feel like pouring some of the earth on to the floor.

Be quiet and experience how these elementals feel. Notice what you sense and what your impressions are. Give thanks.

Water When you are ready, move on. Put the earth down and pick up the water. Hold the water in your hand and contemplate it. Extend your awareness to the elementals of water. Slowly pour some of the water. Greet the water elementals affectionately and invite them to be closer to you.

Be quiet and experience how these elementals feel. Notice what you sense and what your impressions are. Give thanks.

Air When you are ready, move on again. Put the water down and pick up the fan or feather. Hold it in your hand and contemplate it. Extend your awareness to the elementals of air. Move the fan or feather so as to create a breeze. Greet the air elementals affectionately and invite them to be closer to you. Be quiet and experience how these elementals feel. Notice what you sense and what your impressions are. Give thanks.

Fire When you are ready, move on. Put the fan or feather down and pick up the candle or lamp. Hold it in your hand and contemplate it. Extend your awareness to the elementals

of fire. Light the flame. Greet the fire elementals affectionately and invite them to be closer to you. Be quiet and
experience how these elementals feel. Notice what you sense
and what your impressions are. Give thanks.

Now sit quietly and be aware of all four elements. Imagine
them in a circle around you. If it feels comfortable for you,
imagine one element in each of the four directions – north,
south, east and west. (You may have a preference for where
each should sit. It varies in different traditions.)
   Contemplate the atmosphere. When you are ready to end,
give thanks and communicate to the elementals that they can
depart.
   Gently end the exercise.

Landscape Spirits

Wherever you travel in the landscape there are new spirits, and
connecting with them is a standard procedure for experienced
trekkers and pilgrims. It is common practice when arriving at a
new place to make some kind of gift to the local spirits. In many
traditions it is the custom to give grain or some other food or
herb, often gracefully thrown or scattered with an elegant sweep
of the hand. It is a gesture of respect and relationship. On
pilgrimages to some sacred sites, such as Mount Kailas in Tibet,
people may stop and kiss the ground every ten paces in order to
show respect.
   But it is not simply a matter of good manners. By coming into
relationship with a landscape deva, you allow your own energy
field to sense and absorb the local patterns. In unknown terrain
this can be crucial, particularly in bad weather. There are many
stories of angry mountains throwing off visitors with foul weather,
but welcoming and befriending those who stop to make an offering and create relationship with the spirits of the place.
Experienced tribal people would rather turn around than ignore
the spirits in landscape.

Mount Shasta in northern California is notorious for rejecting walkers and climbers who do not treat her and her spirits with respect and make offerings. Over and over again, disrespectful visitors are greeted by unseasonal winds, showers and snowstorms which turn them back, occasionally fatally. In England, one arrogant spiritual teacher climbed Glastonbury Tor, thinking that he would extend a significant blessing to the world from its peak. As he neared the top, however, a sudden gust of wind knocked him off balance and he fell, breaking his leg.

It is obvious that connecting with the appropriate spirit and then allowing yourself to follow its guidance, to be intuitively led by it, is a wonderful way of exploring landscape. In a strange land, it is also a way of feeling companionship.

This tradition of gifting has carried over into many towns and cities where people still throw coins into fountains and wells, greeting the water spirit of the place. Connecting with the local spirit brings luck.

OFFERING TO A LANDSCAPE SPIRIT

When you come to a new place or a place that has a special interest for you, pause before you fully enter the landscape. Come to centre and allow your awareness to go out to the spirits of the place. Pause again and allow yourself to notice any impressions you receive.

Then greet the spirits politely and with a sense of gratitude. Inform them aloud or telepathically that you are entering their landscape and that you hope this meets with their approval. As a gesture of your recognising them, make your offering. Do it calmly and sincerely.

Pause again to contemplate the area and notice any thoughts or senses. If you have no absolutely clear sense of being told to turn around, begin to go forward.

Give thanks.

Fairies, Elves and Tree Angels

Let's go straight into the exercise.

FAIRIES, ELVES AND TREE ANGELS

Do this at home or outside. Sit quietly and go into centred silence. Be aware of the life and moving energy that is in and through your body.

Gradually extend your awareness to include a blade of grass. The very fabric of the blade is made up of atoms, molecules and sparkling deva essence. The blade as a whole has its own tiny grass elemental accompanying it. Smile at it. Greet it. Notice how you feel and what your impressions are.

Widen your perspective now so that you have awareness of a patch of grass. This is a small ocean of green life, dancing with tiny deva life. Greet it all. Notice how you feel and what your impressions are.

Become aware now of the flowers and the smaller plants. Be aware of their fairies and little spirits. Greet them. Be grateful for their presence. Stay calm and allow impressions to come to you.

Move on now to larger plants and go through the same procedure.

Finally, move on to the trees and go through the same procedure.

Contemplate the whole experience. Do you have any impressions of what you might do to cement the relationship? Make an offering? Do something special with plants? If you do have an impression like that, commit yourself to doing it.

Give thanks and bring the exercise to an end.

The Landscape in General

It is obviously life-enhancing to be aware of your local landscape, nature spirits and landscape angels. I encourage friends and students to obtain detailed maps of where they live and work. It is also useful, especially if you live in a built-up area, to get some maps drawn when the place was still undeveloped.

Looking at these maps, you can catch a real sense of the contours of the landscape. Notice where there is or was natural

water, and where there are hills and slopes. Be aware of all the
spirits that inhabit your locality.

Ideally, before anyone interfered with landscape or did new
building or garden design, they would attune to the local landscape, plants, animals and spirits. It is well known, for example,
that nature spirits, even in the most beautifully designed garden,
still like a small wild area. Marko Pogacnik, a Slovenian sculptor
and student of landscape spirits, has said, 'If fields are to retain
their fertility, they must retain their wild hedges. Without these
hedges there is nowhere left for the gnomes and elementals of
growth to anchor into the locality. Crops will grow but they will
lack real vitality.'

There are schools of gardening and horticulture, such as
permaculture and the approaches of anthroposophy, which give
clear awareness to the needs of the nature spirits. The Findhorn
Foundation spearheaded a renaissance of this awareness in
Europe and the United States. The basic approach acknowledges
that the earth is a living being, as is everything else involved in
these people's horticulture. Spirits of all kinds – Pans, plant
spirits, gnomes and spirits of the weather – are relevant to their
work. They also recognise the importance of the general cycles of
nature – the rhythm of the seasons and the phases of the moon.
They take all of this into account when planning and imple-
menting their farming. Needless to say, the process is completely
organic – no artificial fertilisers are used, and the resulting
vegetables radiate vital energy and good health. And the flowers
are stunning. When I am in these places I can feel the land radiating goodwill.

COOPERATING WITH LANDSCAPE SPIRITS

This exercise assumes that you are about to do some building,
or to change your garden or landscape in some way. First
spend some time researching and looking at holistic models of
garden design, house building and town planning. Make sure
that you are aware of the different possibilities.

When you are ready, go quiet and come to centre. Gently
begin to contemplate the work that you are going to do. Give

yourself plenty of time for this. Contemplate what outcome is really needed.

Then let your mind become aware of the landscape in which the work will happen. Spend a while sensing it. Watch the contours of the land. Contemplate the kind of soil, and the rock or clay beneath it. Be aware of the plant and animal life.

Gently become aware of the spirits that are part of this whole community. Greet them warmly and gratefully acknowledge their presence. Spend a while just sensing them. Notice if you are guided to make any special gesture to them. If it feels right, make this gesture.

Contemplate their lives and become their companion.

Do this exercise several times until you feel comfortably familiar with the environment and its beings. Only go on to the next part when you feel you have a rapport with them.

Again, go into contemplation and attunement. Then, when you feel connected, communicate to the spirits, telepathically or aloud, that you are intending to do your building or gardening in their space. Apologise for the disturbance and communicate that you are open to their advice.

Sit quietly and notice what you feel and what your impressions are. Under normal circumstances you will feel a great willingness on their part to cooperate. You will also feel resistance in certain areas, for example from the gnomes of particular trees. You will need to feel your way into some comfortable agreement.

Do this exercise several times. Take serious note of the impressions you receive.

If you find that some of the spirits are totally resistant, but you still have to carry on with your building or landscape work, you will need to call in a greater spirit.

Go through all the procedures described above and become aware of the resistant spirits. Apologise to them. Then contemplate the fact that there is a landscape angel, a healing Pan, who will help the spirits who are in distress. Connect with this healing angel, call it in and gratefully acknowledge its presence. Clearly communicate to this angel the distress of the resistant spirit. Apologise and ask the angel to help move the distressed spirit on. You must remember that the distressed spirit is magnetically attached to its place and has difficulty releasing itself until its blueprint is fulfilled.

Be aware of the angel helping and healing the lesser spirit. Be very grateful. Again, after contemplating the situation, you may feel called to make some gesture of thanks or compensation. If so, do so.

If you find yourself working in landscape where clumsy and distressing intrusion has taken place, you may also want to do something that is healing and regenerative.

HEALING LANDSCAPE

Go silent and begin to contemplate the bruised landscape and distressed nature spirits. Extend your awareness with compassion and sympathy. On behalf of humanity, apologise. Let them feel your love and sorrow.

Then, as above, contemplate a healing landscape angel. Attune to that angel, invite it in and gratefully acknowledge its presence. Ask it to overlight and help the landscape.

Sit for a while with the landscape, the spirits and the angel. Contemplate what might be done to bring about some healing. Take serious notice of any impressions or thoughts. You may be asked to plant something in a particular corner; or to create a piece of art which you give to the place; or to sing to it; or to perform some ceremony in it; or to meditate regularly with it; or to channel healing into the place.

You will probably need to repeat this exercise several times in order to feel clear about what needs doing. Then do it. Make apologies and give thanks.

8

The Healing Dimension

THIS CHAPTER LOOKS in a practical way at how you can use your connection with devas for healing yourself and others. Working cooperatively and consciously with healing angels and the body elementals is very effective.

Your Soul as Angel

Before looking at the healing spirits, it is important to understand some of the characteristics of the human soul. Without this, the work of the healing angels will not make sense.

You are more than just your everyday self and personality. Yes, you have a complex and very full personality, created by family and social environment, but you are also something else. Deep within you, permeating every part of you, and often experienced when you are sitting quietly, is who you really are – core, soul, essence.

Your core self, your soul, is very like an angel. It carries the essential blueprint for who you really are, the pattern for your perfect fulfilment. Your soul holds the notes, tones and colours for how your life can perfectly be, and this is surely angelic.

THE RELATIONSHIP BETWEEN SOUL AND HEALTH

This idea is directly relevant to illness and healing, because real health consists of an energetic harmony between your soul's blueprint and how you express and live your daily life. Your challenge, as a human being caught in all the stimulation of life, is to allow the blueprint of your soul to come into your daily experience. But, because human psychological and social life is so complex, this is not easy to do. We all behave in ways that ignore the pattern of our souls.

This conflict causes friction and irritation, and eventually illness. Energy, emotions, feelings and thoughts stop flowing healthily. Coagulation, inertia and resistance begin to form in your energy body and psyche.

When illness of any kind manifests in you, some part of your system has begun to go into a dysfunctional state. Its energy does not flow smoothly and healthily. It begins to contract, and to transform in malignant and uncomfortable ways. This can happen in any part of the system – from one tiny cell through to the whole psychological personality.

The actual illness can be seen as a tragedy or a blessing. It is a tragedy if you do not understand what is going on and feel that you are a victim. It is a blessing if you understand that the illness is a signal and a lesson on how to bring your life into greater harmony with your soul.

Charles was a medical psychiatrist whose essence clearly held a pattern of service through kindness, intelligence and understanding. As a practitioner he was kind and insightful, but he was always impatient for results and at home and socially his attitudes were self-centred and aggressive.

This psychological dynamic set up an inner friction that finally anchored as cancer of the colon. During his slow convalescence after surgery, he became more gentle, thoughtful and kind. During this phase, his daily personality was in harmony with his soul's pattern and his cancer did not grow. But as he regained his strength and vitality he slipped back into his old ways. Indignant about the illness, be became self-pitying and aggressive once more. Again, there was dissonance between his soul and his expression. And again, the cancer began to grow. He repeated this pattern three times, but he still could not learn the lesson. To have healed, he would have needed to surrender to the patterns of his essence.

Here is another, very different, case. Louise's inner pattern was to be extrovert, positive and in a leadership role. She was also a very sensitive healer. Because of her psychological insecurity, however, she was unable to express herself fully and kept herself contained and controlled. This friction between her soul's pattern and her daily expression began to clog up the flow of her energy system. She lost vitality and became very exhausted. At the same time, the energy that should have been flowing mentally began to coagulate around the brain and she began to experience great psychological distress. After four years of severe crisis, she started to understand and accept that she was a 'big' woman. A healthy healing process began.

Group Karma and Accidents

The kind of illnesses described above are all the result of inner psychological friction. But, despite the beliefs of some New Age Circles, not all illnesses are caused in this way. There is a danger-ous fallacy that people are responsible for everything that happens to them and that every illness is a deserved lesson. This attitude fails to appreciate the larger context or the real ways of the world.

If a toddler falls and scrapes her knee, there is no point in looking for inner psychological frictions. What we have here is a little human creature learning to walk and run. The wound needs washing and dressing, and the child needs cuddles and care. Adults, too, are prone to accidents. We are all tumbling around this small planet with six billion other souls. Accidents are bound to happen in a complex environment.

There are also many situations when people are caught up in a tide of mass events. Epidemics, genocide and wars are all exam-ples of large group events in which individuals may get caught up regardless of their own will. People who are physically or psycho-logically weak will be most at risk in these situations.

Much of the present-day cancer, for example, is due not to inner psychic coagulation but to the huge and thoughtless increase in the use of artificial fertilisers and chemical food additives, and in pollution and radiation. Those with the weakest constitutions fall victim first. Similarly, children dying because of famine have no choice in their situation. They are victims of mass events.

This will be obvious to most sensible people, but I state it clearly here because of the current trend of asserting that everyone creates their own reality and nothing happens by chance. While these ideas are partly true, they should not be seen as a universal interpretation. But whether the cause of the illness is personal disharmony or bad fortune, the process of healing is always the same: love, care, empathy and the ability to get healing energy flowing healthily back within the system.

The Holistic Approach

Modern Western medicine usually advocates a mechanical response: if a headache, then a painkiller. While this is sometimes humane and appropriate, the mechanical approach excludes the inner condition of the patient and does not catch the holistic pattern – personal history, physiology, family, emotions, mind-set, personality type and so on. A holistic approach necessarily includes a sensitive attunement, which is why so many healers, therapists and practitioners of alternative medicine are working with angels whether they know it or not.

What are Healing Angels?

What we are talking about here is those devas who have long experience of involvement with humanity and know the basic patterns of human development and growth. They understand the patterns for a healthy human body and the way these are intimately linked and attuned to the emotional and mental patterns. Their own history started as elemental life in the human energy field.

Because of their open awareness to perfect fulfilment, they are also fully aware of the human soul. They completely understand the dynamics of the soul–personality relationship, and that most illness is the result of the friction between the personality patterns and the soul's intended music. This means that a healing angel is aware of the two major realities in illness:

- The actual distress and possibilities for healing in the physical, energetic and psychological bodies.
- The dynamic of the body–soul connection.

Do you already have a Healing Angel?

You might ask whether a healer's compassion, sympathy and love are not enough. Why do you need a healing spirit? In my experience a healer with these qualities is always accompanied by a healing angel anyway. How could a healing angel resist working with such a loving healer?

I have known a number of therapists and doctors who reject the idea of devas and angels but nevertheless are accompanied by healing angels. There is a sensitivity, clarity and care in their work which has the aura and atmosphere of a healing angel's presence. The most mainstream of medical psychiatrists often have a good intuitive sense of how the sessions will work and close. My own psychoanalyst was a tough medical man who frightened people with his intellect and was a determined atheist. He was also a deeply compassionate and sympathetic practitioner, and there was a warm glow around his consulting room which was definitely angelic.

Healing angels are actively looking for opportunities to cooperate with us, and this cooperation is not restricted to trained therapists and healers. Many people today have an interest in counselling and health, and most of us try to be good listeners. In a sense, depending on the situation, we are all healers. And we can all cooperate with healing spirits.

Healers and counsellors nearly always have a sense of how the healing session will end. It is the same when you are helping a distressed friend. You will listen and talk, perhaps touch, in ways to promote the best outcome. You may, for example, have a clear sense that the friend needs to weep or get angry before he or she feels better. So you guide the conversation and try different strategies to achieve this end.

In a way this is very angelic. You have a sense of the pattern for that healing. You know the blueprint, and you work to build a bridge and create that outcome. This is the essence of good healing work – a sensitive awareness of the situation and the possible outcome. Then you use your particular skills to bridge it into being fulfilled.

Is there a healing angel already accompanying you or a particular healer? Go quiet. What do you sense? Is there a certain stillness and magic and grace in the atmosphere? What does your own energy body feel? What is your intuition? Do you have a sense of happy apprehension before doing healing work? Do you look forward to it?

There is a beautiful North American Kwakiutl prayer to the healing spirit:

> *I beg you, supernatural power, that you take pity and make well this our friend.*
> *I implore you, Supernatural Power, that you take pity and take out this sickness of this our friend, Supernatural Power.*
> *Oh take pity that I may make alive this our friend. O Supernatural Power that I may cure this our friend you go through, Supernatural Power.*
> *That I may obtain easily this sickness of our friend, O Great Supernatural Power, you great Life-Bringer, Supernatural Power, you great Life-Bringer, Supernatural Power.*

WORKING WITH HEALING ANGELS: THE BASICS

The mechanics of working with a healing angel are very straightforward. In a healing situation, your energy field connects with and feels the aura of the person who needs help. Your field senses the energy patterns and blockages. You also feel your client's soul and the blueprint that it is trying to manifest.

The healing angel is also aware of these dynamics and, because of its history and experience, knows the best way in which energies can be made to flow and vibrate in order to bring appropriate healing. The healing angel holds the pattern of this healing process over the situation.

You, the healer, are therefore connected both with the pattern of your client and with the energetic blueprint of the angel. In your calm attunement to the needs of the situation, your aura feels all this.

You work with healing angels in precisely the same way that you work with all other spirits: attunement, invitation, action. Your attitude, as ever, will be quiet and attentive, noticing subtle impressions and the hints of direction and guidance. That last sentence, appropriate to any situation in which you cooperate with spirits, is particularly so when describing a good healer, counsellor or therapist.

And then of course, in your own way, you have to act. A talk therapist listens and guides the conversation with intuited questions and comments. An osteopath or chiropractor has a sense of how the body energies can be moved and released by particular kinds of touch and movement. A spiritual healer will channel energy of a particular quality to a particular area.

A New Kind of Physiology

Before looking more closely at how to work with healing angels, you need to know more about the constitution of the physical body – in particular those elementals and spirits which are interwoven with the physical and energy body.

Western medicine is gradually being introduced to alternative models of physiology, particularly from Chinese and Ayurvedic medicine which has a clear understanding of the energy and energy centres of the human body. But there is little awareness, as yet, of the deva element that is in every body. Yet there are as many devas as there are biological and energetic bits and pieces.

In any illness or disease, the perfect pattern envisaged and held by the relevant spirit is being obstructed and cannot fulfil itself. The kidney elemental, for example, may be blocked from magnetically drawing the kidney itself into its perfect state. In many animist and tribal religions in which everything, animate and inanimate, is perceived to have life, the correctly named 'medicine men' speak directly to the spirits of the diseased organs.

In the same way that medical professionals have to familiarise themselves with anatomy, if you wish to work with healing devas you must get to know the elemental life of the body. Particular organs and aspects of the body must be seen and understood as beings in their own right.

SENSING THE PHYSICAL BODY ELEMENTALS

Get comfortable and go quiet in the way that works best for you.

Begin to turn your awareness down into your body. Have a warm and affectionate attitude towards your internal organs. Feel a gentle warmth running through your stomach and inside your chest.

When you feel ready, turn your attention to any part of your body that attracts your attention. If there is no area in particular that you are drawn to, focus on one of your fingers. Take your focus into the skin of a fingertip and imagine that you are like a very powerful microscope, looking closer and closer and closer.

Finally you are looking at just one atom. It is a dancing, spinning cosmos of particles and waves, and accompanying it is an elemental who holds its perfect pattern and bridges it into being. Greet that tiny deva. Contemplate its beauty and its work.

When you feel like it, bring your attention away from that single atom and become aware of the millions of atoms that make up your entire body. Notice how your whole body is a shimmering system of these atoms.

This entire system has a single deva who is its companion and holds the blueprint of perfect physical health for you. This being is sometimes called the Body Elemental. Greet it affectionately. Contemplate its beauty and its work.

Then, in your own time, take your awareness into any aspect, any organ, of your body – a lung, the bone marrow, the skeleton, a particular bone, the circulatory system, the endocrine system, the immune system – and become aware that this aspect too has its own devic companion and living blueprint. Greet it affectionately. Contemplate its beauty and its work.

Over a period of time, repeat this exercise many times, becoming familiar with your physical body, its different parts and its elementals.

The human body is, of course, not just a physical vehicle. Vitality or prana moves around and through it, and there are also the whirlpools of energy, the centres known in Ayurvedic medicine as chakras. There are seven major chakras, located between the base of the spine and the top of the head. Each chakra is a spinning centre of emotion and mental energy which anchor down into the physical body.

SENSING THE ENERGY BODY ELEMENTALS

Get comfortable and go quiet in the way that works best for you.

Begin to turn your awareness down into your body. Have a warm and affectionate attitude towards your internal organs. Feel a gentle warmth running through your stomach and inside your chest.

Gradually allow yourself to become aware of the energy that is running and circulating through your body. It runs beneath the skin, deep into the bone marrow and out into your wider energy field. Affectionately greet this energy system and become aware of the spirit who holds its perfect pattern.

Gratefully acknowledge this spirit. Sit quietly and notice what you feel and any thoughts.

Then, when you are ready, gradually turn your attention to the energy of your emotions. This too is all around and through you. Notice its different characteristics, its range of moods. Greet it affectionately and become aware of the spirit who holds its perfect pattern. Gratefully acknowledge this spirit. Sit quietly and notice what you feel and any thoughts.

Again, when you are ready, gradually turn your attention to the energy of your mental body. This too is all around and through you. Notice its different characteristics, its range of ideas and attitudes. Greet it affectionately and become aware of the spirit who holds its perfect pattern. Gratefully acknowledge this spirit. Sit quietly and notice what you feel and any thoughts.

Then, when you are ready, gradually turn your attention to the chakras that run up your body. The base of your spine. Around your sexual organs. The solar plexus. The throat. The brow. The crown. Be aware of all seven of them as a complete system and that each of them is also unique. Be aware that they are made up of physical, emotional and mental energy. Greet them affectionately. Become aware that there is an elemental who works with each chakra and with the whole system.

Depending on how you feel and where your focus goes most easily, greet and gratefully acknowledge the presence of the elemental of each chakra. Focus on one in particular, or give attention in a flow to each one.

Again, do this exercise as often as you want to increase your intimacy, awareness and relationship with your energy body and its elemental beings. If focussing on all the different parts in one session is too much for you, just choose particular areas of interest.

Flower Essences and Homeopathy

One of the best ways to connect with healing spirits is through the use of flower essences and homeopathy. Throughout history, many cultures have recognised that different plants carry different harmonics which can be used for healing. In the context of this book you can understand that the blueprint of a plant deva has a certain vibration and tone to it. One plant deva may be particularly appropriate for working with emotional sadness; another works with mental judgements. The vibration and blueprint of the deva have a certain spin which works 'musically' to take the distress into a new and more flowing vibration. The physical body benefits from the actual chemicals in plants, but there is also the effect of the plant's deva and blueprint. This is precisely why flower essences and homeopathic remedies work.

Many people cannot understand how homeopathy works, since the original physical constituent of the medication is so diluted that scientific instruments can find no trace of it. But the homeopathic remedy still contains the blueprint of the plant or mineral. The energetic structure of a homeopathic pill carries the devic essence, and it is the same with flower essences. So when you take these remedies you are taking into your body the energetic blueprint of the plant spirit. And because this is connected harmonically with the other elementals and angels of their species you are also bringing into your body a connection with the whole field of relevant devas.

This connection spins a new vibration into your energy body, which works harmonically with the elements of the sickness and the elementals of the relevant organs. It is a wonderful and very grounded way to make use of the healing vibrations of plant spirits.

Working with Healing Angels: Forging a Relationship

The following series of exercises will bring you into working relationship with healing angels.

TO HAVE A RELATIONSHIP WITH A HEALING ANGEL

Do this exercise before seeing your friends or clients. Do it regularly in order to create a relationship.

Go centred and calm in the way that works best for you.

Begin to imagine yourself in a healing situation. You are with your client or friend who needs your healing help. Imagine that there is an angel overlighting the situation with a warm and helpful energy. This angel knows perfectly how the healing can take place. This angel's energy envelops your companion and you. Imagine yourself covered by this angel's light.

Then in your own words, aloud or telepathically, ask for this healing angel to come to you. Feel it coming into your presence. Gratefully acknowledge its presence. Ask for it to stay with you and be with you whenever you are in a healing situation. Thank it.

Stay quiet, contemplating its presence and the implications for future situations. Notice what passes through your mind and what you feel.

When you are ready to end this exercise, communicate to the angel that it can either stay with you or go, whichever it wants, but ask that it be with you when you need it. Again, express gratitude.

Gently come out of the exercise.

CONNECTING WITH YOUR ANGEL JUST BEFORE HEALING

When you are in the healing situation, before you do anything with your friend or client, take a little while to be quiet. If you are embarrassed by this, you could say something to your friend like, 'Do you mind if I stop for a little while to think about what we have here? I just want to focus my mind properly.'

Bring yourself to centre.

Recognise that your energy body extends to connect with and include the energy body of your client. Envisage that over you and surrounding both of you is the aura of a healing angel.

Invite this angel to be with you and thank it for its presence. Stay quiet a while longer and allow the connection to be fully absorbed by you. Let the angel's aura into you. Notice what images, instincts or thoughts you have. Know that the healing work you are about to do is inevitably moving towards a healthy fulfilment.

Then, when you are ready, move instinctively into the kind of therapy you do.

If at any point you become uncertain about what is happening or what you should do next, go back into your inner calm. Centre. Connect again with the overlighting angel. Begin again.

When the session is over, give thanks.

The object of the next exercise is to discover a spirit whose blueprint is of help to you in your general health. You can do it as often as you like, and you will find that the spirits will change through time.

OUTSIDE HEALING AGENTS

Bring yourself to calm in the way that best suits you.

Look down into your body with affectionate love. Greet the different parts and elementals of your body. Be aware of their dancing life.

Gently let your awareness open to nature and the universe. Let your mind go wandering through fields, hills and mountains. Let your awareness move into forests and oceans. Let it open also to the heavens.

Contemplate that nature and the universe are full of life and spirits. Appreciate and be thankful for this richness and beauty.

Stay very relaxed and see where your attention is particularly drawn. There may be a particular plant, animal, star or planet that attracts you. If there is, let your focus rest on it for a while. Greet it affectionately and be aware that there is also an accompanying spirit. Connect with this spirit and acknowledge its existence.

Ask this spirit to allow an elemental part of it to come into your energy field. Stay quiet and feel and sense it. Allow it to come into your body. Feel its effect. Imagine this new inner relationship bringing you a quality of new healing and greater health.

Relax and allow the exercise to fall away from you.

Give thanks.

Afterwards you may want to research whatever you connected with in the exercise. If it was a plant or animal or star, you might want to read about it or find a picture of it to put up somewhere. This helps to perpetuate the relationship.

If you have an instinctive feeling for this kind of spirit work, you can begin to focus on a friend's or client's body elementals.

First, do everything in the preceding exercise.

When you are calm and feel the overlighting presence of the healing angel, turn your attention to the particular organ or body area or energy with which you are working. (This can be as general as the spinal column or as specific as an individual disc. It can also, for instance, be the whole emotional body or a particular organ.) Recognise that this body part has its own elemental counterpart.

Affectionately greet the elemental of the area with which you are working. Thankfully acknowledge its presence.

Telepathically communicate that you are very sympathetic to its situation. It holds the perfect pattern, but a friction or blockage in the energy field is stopping it from fulfilling its perfect purpose. Ask what it needs in order to be brought back into healthy flow.

Contemplate and notice any impressions. Be open to what passes through your mind and what you instinctively and intuitively sense. At the very least, you know that it wants love, warmth and a sense of healthy movement.

Then, if you have clarity, do what is appropriate.

Again, if at any point your are unclear what to do, calm yourself and come back into attunement with the elemental.

When you feel complete, gently bring the session to a close. Give thanks.

Pathological Elementals

Even diseased parts of the body have devic essence within them. Any part of the physical or energy body that is ill contains elementals which are part of that particular illness. In their own appropriate place, in other situations, they do no harm – but in the sick area of the body they are not wanted.

It is possible to communicate directly with these elementals and to ask them to transform or move on their way. Tribal medicine men would dance, sing, shake rattles, spit herbs or use fire to get these elementals to move on, but you will probably prefer the following exercise.

COMMUNICATING WITH PATHOLOGICAL ELEMENTALS

Do this in the context of a proper healing. First of all go through the procedure described above for calling in and connecting with the healing.

When you feel absolutely centred and have called in the healing angel, then go ahead with this exercise.

Gently begin to attune to the elementals associated with the actual illness. These may be physical elementals lodged in the body or elementals of subtler energy in prana or the emotions or mind.

Be aware that, as you connect with these elementals, you may find the experience uncomfortable or unpleasant. This is because your energy field is actually feeling the vibration and the resonance of the pathological elementals.

If you do feel anxious, end the exercise.

If, however, you feel anxious but are nevertheless called to this kind of work, engage with it very gradually, on a step-by-step basis. Bring yourself into connection with the sickness elementals for only a few seconds the first times you make contact, and gradually extend your connection until you feel confident and comfortable.

When you feel attuned to the sickness elementals, greet them affectionately and thank them for being present. Then gently begin to imagine how they might transform or move on. Contemplate their transformation and removal. Allow yourself to sense and intuit what you need to do to help the process.

At the very least, the energy of your loving attention will help them release from their attachment.

In this kind of a situation, you need to be prepared for many different kinds of strategies, some of which might be creatively aggressive. For example, you might find yourself thinking of using a cleansing incense, or powerful vibrations, or intense prayers and energy.

This is very delicate work. Do not act on anything unless you feel certain of the presence of the overlighting healing angel and until you have carefully reflected on whether the course of action feels wise and creative. If you feel clear, go ahead.

Before ending the session, go into the energy of the healing angel. Then feel cleansing energy moving healthily through and around you.

Give thanks to all the spirit beings involved.

Gently close the session.

In *Brotherhood of Angels and Men* Geoffrey Hodson offers a very useful healing invocation:

> *Hail, devas of the healing art!*
> *Come to our aid.*
> *Pour forth your healing life*
> *Into this [person or place]*
> *Let every cell be charged anew*
> *With vital force.*
> *To every nerve give peace.*
> *Let tortured sense be soothed.*
> *May the rising tide of life*
> *Set every limb aglow,*
> *As, by your healing power,*
> *Both soul and body are restored.*
> *Leave here an angel watcher,*
> *To comfort and protect,*
> *Till health returns or life departs,*
> *That he may ward away all ill,*
> *May hasten the returning strength –*
> *Or lead to peace when life is done.*
> *Hail, devas of the healing art!*
> *Come to our aid,*
> *And share with us the labours of this earth,*
> *That spirit may be set free in all.*

The Universal Connection

In general, the dynamic for healing is always the same – bring your outer expression into harmony with your true inner blueprint. There is also an environmental context for the healing process. You and your body are not isolated: you are part of a much greater universe. And connection with the universe creates a healing harmonic, a recipe for perfect health. Separation is a powerful part of all illness.

There is no huge cosmic blueprint saying that failing and unhappiness are the perfect fulfilment for you. On the contrary, it is full of love and hope and creativity. Without exception, when people connect with the wider dimension they know-feel-understand-experience that everything is wonderful. It is obviously a fundamental part of good health to feel this connection.

Spirits live perpetually in this universal connection. Even when they are intimately associated with human activity, they are still part of the wider flow. So when you connect with the spirit world you are also opening yourself to the way devas experience life. Connecting with angels opens a doorway for you into this greater, clearer and more loving dimension. This means that simply being aware of spirits is healing.

ANGEL OF UNIVERSAL CONNECTION

Get comfortable and go quiet in the way that works best for you.

Begin to contemplate the beauty of nature and the universe. Think of all the places, plants and creatures you love. Think of the beautiful people you know. Think of the stars and heavens. Contemplate how lovely nature is.

Recognise that there is a beautiful spirit who knows perfectly how you can feel relaxed and connected to the inner world. This is your Angel of Universal Connection. Spend a while contemplating the existence of such an angel.

When you are ready, call it in and express gratitude for its presence. Ask it to be with you all the time, helping and strengthening your connection with the beauty of all life, with God, with spirit.

Be quiet a while longer and notice what you feel and your impressions.

The Healing Support of All Spirits

Connecting consciously with devas in general also supports self-healing by enhancing the magnetism of your own body elementals and strengthening the blueprint of your health. The easiest and most effective way of doing this is to connect with spirits associated with the people, places and activities that you really love. This way you can be sure to bring in a creative and supportive vibration.

CONNECTING WITH A SUPPORTIVE SPIRIT

Before you do this exercise think of the people, places and activities that you love, which comfort and inspire you. (If possible, do this exercise physically close to them.)

Go quiet in your own comfortable way.

Once you have settled, turn your attention to your own body, its different parts and its energy system. Greet them affectionately and greet the elementals that accompany your body.

If you have a particular illness, affectionately greet the place in your body where that illness manifests. Then greet the elemental or elementals that accompany that body region.

Now gently turn your attention to the person, situation or activity that you really love. Let your awareness play with memories of it. Connect with it. Greet it affectionately.

Go on to contemplate the spirit that accompanies it. Attune to that spirit. Invite it to connect with you.

Then begin to imagine a comfortable and harmonic energy running between this spirit and the elementals of your body. Very gently envisage your body elementals enjoying and being strengthened by this relationship.

Contemplate and sense the good feeling that may now begin to move through your body, especially where there is illness. This is healing for you.

Experience the magic sparkling energy of your body and its elementals. Feel the ill areas being open to a new dance of fulfilled health.

Thank the deva that you invited in for its companionship and support. Ask it to continue supporting your body elemental.

Gradually withdraw from the exercise.

There is an important general point here. The kind of calm you need to connect with spirits is exactly the kind of calm and relaxation that nurtures your healing process anyway.

You should also consider the immense difference between a person who does something attuned to the spirit of their activity and a person who has no awareness. Are you living and working in a way that is generally attuned to the spirits of your life? Or are you unaware? The following exercise will help you.

ARE YOU ATTUNED TO THE SPIRIT OF YOUR ACTIVITIES?

Go into silence in the way that suits you best.

When you feel centred, begin to survey the main activities in your life. Your family. Your relationships. Your work. Your hobbies. Your leisure. All the main activities.

Just watch them calmly.

Choose the main work that you do. Staying calm and affectionately watching yourself, ask whether you are connected with the spirit of the activity. Is the way you do this work in harmony with how you really want to do it?

Look at the style, atmosphere and sensation of your actions.

Have no judgements on yourself, whatever the answer. If you are a frantic speed freak, or if you get overwhelmed, or if you are lazy, just notice and smile philosophically.

Then begin to contemplate how it might be if you were attuned to the spirit of the activity. If you invited in the spirit and attuned to it, how might your activities be?

Spend a while gently contemplating these questions. Allow any and all images and thoughts to surface. Then, when you are ready, gently bring the contemplation to an end.

From the exercises that have already appeared in this book, you know how to call in the appropriate spirit and work cooperatively with it – if you want to.

Just contemplating all this is healthy because it begins to open up your relationships with the relevant devas. Asking these questions, remembering that you need to attune to the spirit of what you are doing, starts to bring you into a new experience of your activities.

Spirits in Need of Healing

The context of healing is the right place to address the issue of negative devas.

Let me assert first of all that in my opinion there is no such thing as an essentially negative or evil spirit. There are, however, devas who carry negative vibrations and patterns which they have absorbed from human behaviour.

When obsessive, neurotic and selfish people use their own animal magnetism to call devas into intimate cooperation with them, a small deva such as an elf or cherub of ceremony can be drawn away from its natural open connection with the matrix of other devas and the benevolent universe. In these situations, the power of the human personality becomes like God for the deva, which begins to absorb the patterns of this person.

Imagine a ritualist or healer who is self-obsessed, cruel and sexually perverse. To begin with, the small healing or ceremonial spirit comes in to help in the normal way. But the individual's obsessiveness creates an energy field which does not release the deva. Unable to disengage, the spirit absorbs the atmosphere and imprint of the corrupt attitude and actions into its blueprint of possibilities. A ritualist might, for example, use ceremony to gratify sexual lust or a desire for sadistic behaviour. The spirit absorbs that pattern.

If that spirit is released, it still carries the imprint that it has absorbed. Anybody who comes close to this spirit will feel that imprint. And if someone who is weak-willed connects with that corrupted deva, there is a possibility that the person may well be influenced, or at least frightened, by the deva's vibration.

Many years ago I was called in to help somebody living in a basement flat in central London who was experiencing unpleasant phenomena. The atmosphere would suddenly become very frightening and spooky and he would feel electric shocks around his back and shoulders. Lights flickered in the dark and he had uncontrollable hallucinations of pools of blood. Inexplicable marks appeared on mirrors and walls.

When I arrived, the atmosphere was indeed horrible. Certain ritual artefacts owned by the infamous occultist Aleister Crowley had been stored in the flat. Along with his cape and ceremonial sword were some ritual devas who had absorbed a lot of human depravity from their experiences. I cleansed the flat (for further advice see my book *Psychic Protection*) and then went into a long cleansing meditation. I let my awareness envelope the whole apartment and gradually drew the unfortunate spirits close to me. I sat with them in my aura for a long time, absorbing their human negativity, and then asked for a healing angel to take them away for convalescence.

The flat was perfectly fine after that. I do not know what happened to the cape and sword.

So the good news is that, since the negative imprint will always have been created by human behaviour, it can also be cleansed by a human being and the deva can be rescued from corruption. The technique for healing a spirit damaged in this way is quite simple, but it is uncomfortable and there are only a few people who do this kind of cleansing work. The method is given below, but if you do not feel confident, do not even consider it!

HEALING A DAMAGED SPIRIT

As always, go calm and centred in the way that suits you best.

Make sure that you feel perfectly centred and connected to the benevolence and love in the universe.

Contemplate a special kind of healing angel who fully understands all the energies involved in cleansing and redeeming a damaged spirit. Call in this spirit and gratefully acknowledge its presence. Call in any other spirits with whom you are familiar and who will support you.

Then slowly extend your energy field to include the corrupted deva. Your attitude should be affectionate, very strong and very parental. Your vibration should be that of loving compassion.

Invite in and feel the deva in your energy field. Then gently bring it right into your physical body.

Obviously this may not be a pleasant experience. Stay calm, detached and loving, and keep your breath calm and rhythmic. Relax into fully experiencing the poor spirit's corruption. Smile into the corruption and know that by experiencing it you are also transforming it. You can use one of the Buddhist declarations of compassionate meditation: I breathe in negativity, I breathe out blessing.

You may feel your body shudder as it re-vibrates the negative energy. You may have feelings, images and thoughts that relate to the corruption. Stay detached, watchful and loving.

Sense the deva being cleansed and released. When you feel that you have completed the process, ask the healing devas (whom you called in at the beginning) to take away the cleansed deva for a period of further healing and convalescence.

Give thanks. Experience the cleansing energy of nature and the universe running through you. Ask your spirits to check that there is nothing adhering to you. If there is, either absorb it into a transformative process or send it on. Imagine tidal waves of positive energy moving it on from you.

Gently come out of the process. Do whatever you normally do for self-cleansing. Change your clothes. Open the windows. Have a shower or scented bath. Go for a walk.

Give thanks.

9

Working with Angels
That Help Humanity

This chapter looks at those angels that are particularly relevant both to individuals and to groups of people. This includes not only the personal guardian spirits, but also those that work more generally with cities and in civilisation, and those involved in religious ceremony, as well as animal and plant spirits, known as totems.

Personal Guardian Angels

Confusion has arisen here because of stories of angels directly intervening in the material world. An accident is about to happen, and a beautiful being manifests to prevent it. But these interventions are not made by devas or angels. They are made by disincarnate human beings – people without physical bodies – who cannot bear to remain passive observers to some tragedy. In the passion of the moment, these human spirits find the force and will to manifest directly into the material world and give help.

True personal guardian angels are spirits who have long, deep experience of human life. In the same way that a sprite, mermaid or Neptune emerges from the ocean environment, so a guardian angel has emerged from the energy fields of human experience. The main blueprint in its awareness is how to fulfil perfectly the healthy relationship between an individual and his or her soul. Guardian angels want to help you truly fulfil yourself.

The guardian angel understands that you are not just a physical, social and psychological person. You are also who you are in essence, your core self, your soul. And the angel appreciates that the purpose of your life is to bring the harmonics of your soul as fully as possible into daily life.

It does not register or care how you appear to the outside world. It does mind what kind of vibration and 'colour' you are. Perhaps you are supposed to feel wealthy and generous. This does not require money, but is a very private feeling. Perhaps you are supposed to be relaxed and very grounded; or earnest and leading. All these varied characteristics come from moods and attitudes within you, and are not created by social circumstances.

Although it accepts you just as you are, whatever your quirks and history, this is not to say that the guardian angel is like a wise therapist. It is an energy being who is aware of your vibrations and harmonics. It is holding a set of energy patterns to help you play the music of your own unique life.

Your guardian angel carries a very subtle and mellow vibration. If it were obvious you would have noticed it long ago. The most important thing that you can get from feeling connected to your guardian angel is a sense of comfort. It knows you. It loves you. It completely accepts you. If you want, you can envisage it as a great golden being enveloping you in its wings, but it does not carry a sword. Its vibration is more like your favourite cuddly toy from childhood days. As an adult you may receive the same type of comfort from animals or trees or lying on the earth. All of this is very similar to your relationship with your guardian spirit.

MEETING YOUR GUARDIAN ANGEL

This is a very healing exercise which you can do as often as you like. In the way that works best for you, go quiet and centred. If you like, you can do this exercise in bed when you are warm and comfortable.

Allow yourself to curl up energetically and even physically if you want. Turn your attention down into yourself. Be aware only of your own body warmth, your own scent. Take a few gentle deep breaths down as far as possible into your lower belly.

Switch on a gentle and affectionate smile for yourself. Smile down into your body. Greet your organs. Be aware of them.

Energetically collapse into yourself. This is a kind of healthy and nurturing retreat. Especially allow your brain to relax.

Then, when you are ready, begin to contemplate the possibility of having a guardian angel. It accompanies you. It understands the harmonics and challenges between your personality and your essence. It understands and cares for all the different aspects of your physical and energy body.

You do not have to invite it to be present. It is already there. The more you relax, the more you can feel it.

Say hello to it. Greet it. Be open to fully feeling it.

It is there, comforting every single area of your physical and energy body. It soothes your emotions and mind. It knows you so well.

Be passive and completely open to it. In poetic imagery, let the softness of its golden wings hold you.

It is always there.

Be open to any impressions.

When you are ready, say thank you and gently come out of the exercise.

When you have taken yourself into the angel's atmosphere, use that comforting psychic environment to look at any life challenges which need clarifying and healing.

GETTING ADVICE FROM YOUR GUARDIAN ANGEL

Do the exercise above.

When you are feeling comfortable, bring into your awareness the challenge that is troubling you. Stay very comfortable and feel comforted by your angel.

Then ask the angel to help you achieve some clarity about this challenge. It is very important that you stay calm and comforted, and do not get caught up in any anxiety around the issue.

Allow your mind plenty of time to register any impressions. Turn your awareness to possible new strategies. Stay genuinely open to new ideas.

You may have to do this exercise several times before you begin to see some answers.

THE GUARDIAN ANGEL AND YOUR SOUL

Earlier your soul was likened to an angel because it holds the blueprint of who you really are. One of the most fundamental steps on the spiritual path is to realise that you have a soul and that it is the most important part of you. From birth until death it seeks to manifest itself through your personality, and its life continues long after the body and social personality are dust.

The job of your guardian angel is to hold the blueprint of how your soul comes into relationship with your everyday self. The angel, your everyday self and your soul form a triangle, and the angel holds the plan for bringing you into perfect integration, sometimes called the 'mystic marriage'.

Sometimes, in mystical experiences and altered states of consciousness, people open up and feel the full energy and destiny of their souls. This can be a very powerful and life-altering experience, especially as the nervous system and brain register the soul's aura for the first time.

I regularly counsel people who have had this experience and are trying to make sense of it. Sometimes they think that the experience of their own soul was an invisible teacher and saint. Sometimes they think it was God. Both are fully understandable and symbolically true. And people often interpret this experience as coming from their guardian angel.

The soul truly is like an angel, but it rides on different impulses and rhythms. In some traditions the soul is clearly described in angelic images. In the ancient Middle Eastern Sufi tradition, for example, the soul is illustrated as a heart with wings. In Sanskrit texts from further to the East the soul is described as a Solar Angel, an angel from the Sun. And the whole mythic tradition of the fall of the angels can be understood as a description of how the soul, from realms of pure energy, incarnates and descends into the material paradox of human life.

Angels of Death

There is a wonderful group of angels who, when the soul's work is ended for that lifetime, help people die gracefully. They carry in their energy fields the blueprint of the perfect death.

In this blueprint the dying happens with absolutely no fear, but with a graceful and welcoming acceptance of the transition. These angels also hold the energy field so that, as the dying person's consciousness exits from the body, the ride into the next energy field is smooth, safe and encouraging.

Friends, relatives and carers instinctively find themselves behaving in certain ways, such as adopting an attitude of love and caring which may be new for them, that deeply help the dying person to release and move on. This kind of love radiates magnetically from you, reassuring the body elementals of the dying person and creating a sense of grace and easy passing.

When someone close to you is dying you are dealing with two distinct dynamics. The first is grief at the loss of the relative or friend; the second is the transfer of consciousness of the dying person. The major need of both is to feel a reassuring and stable presence, which the angels of death provide from their energy field.

So make sure that you are calm and stable. This brings us back to an instruction repeated throughout the exercises in this book: 'In the way that works for you, go quiet and come to centre.' If you are to be of genuine help when someone is dying, you must be calm, centred, connected to your love and open to cooperating with the spirits of death.

COOPERATING WITH ANGELS OF DEATH

In your own way, go quiet and come to centre.

Make sure that you feel very stable.

Gently expand your awareness to include the dying person. Your attitude and body energy are warm and accepting, relaxed and reassuring.

Recognise that an angel is present who perfectly understands how the process of death happens. This angel carries an aura of great happiness and safety, and will care for the consciousness of the dying person as it comes out of the body and moves on.

Contemplate and gently connect with the presence of this angel. This will be very beautiful.

There are now three distinct ways in which you can help.

Think with great love of your friend and remember the people, the places, the animals, the activities and the spiritual teachers that your friend loved. Telepathically communicate all these to the angel. The angel will then use them to build welcoming images to help your friend across.

Gently ask the angel whether there is anything specific you can do – in terms of prayer and meditation, practical care, contacting relatives and so on – that will help the situation. As always, be quiet and watch your impressions. Then act.

With all the love and spiritual will that you can muster, connect with the great beauty and love and creativity of life. Connect with spirit, with God, with whatever you call the beneficent force that runs through nature and the universe.

When you have this connection with God, expand your energy field to include your dying friend. Have a gentle sense of your energy field helping the dying person to connect with the clear fields of love energy into which she or he will soon be going.

For as long as you can, as often as you can, connect with spirit and extend your energy to your friend. Sense your friend gliding into the clear white light, the angel always helping and caring.

There may be situations in which you have an instinctive sense that there is no angel present to facilitate the passing over. Or perhaps someone has already died, but you sense that they are still present and have not fully made the transition.

CALLING IN AN ANGEL OF DEATH

Go into silence in the way that best suits you.

Extend your awareness to include the person who is dying or has died. Be affectionate and very loving, from your heart, towards this person.

Contemplate the idea that there are angels of death who help people to die. Imagine that such an angel might possibly come to your situation.

Let your telepathic call go gently out in space. Call it in. Ask for an angel of death to be present.

Gratefully acknowledge its presence.

Telepathically communicate to it that there is a situation that needs its help.

Totally trust that the angel can now do everything that is needed.

If you feel like it, help the angel in any of the three ways suggested in the preceding exercise.

Totally trust that all is well.

With gratitude and love, release the exercise.

Angels of Communities

Guardian angels do not just work with individuals, of course. They also look after the places and communities in which we live. In the same way that nature spirits move on to care for larger and more complex forms, so guardian angels also evolve.

In Chapter 3 I described how I first connected with the angel of London, and since then I have come to realise how deeply involved angels are in all human civilisation. To help others arrive at this understanding I have developed the following visualisation exercise which I often use with groups.

THE CITY OF ANGELS

Get very comfortable and go through your usual process of relaxing and coming to centre.

Then imagine that you are lying or sitting in a comfortable and very safe boat. It is floating along in a beautiful blue ocean in the most perfect weather possible. The sun is bright and the temperature is perfect. The boat is being carried on a gentle current.

When you have spent enough time enjoying the sensation of being in the boat, look forward. Far in the distance you can see some snow-capped mountains.

The current gently carries your boat towards the land. As you come closer you can see the mountains in the distance rolling down into soft valleys and gentle green hills, then a green plain that comes down to the ocean.

By the ocean there is a beautiful white city.

From a distance you look at the beauty of the white city. There are companion angels all over it. You can see in the background the angels of the mountains and hills.

This city has a harbour and your boat comes into it. You disembark and are free to wander around the city.

It has a wonderful welcoming atmosphere. Every household has a shrine devoted to its house angel, and over every house you can sense or perceive the deva. At the markets there are shrines dedicated to the goddess of communication and fair exchange, and this angel overlights all transactions. At every theatre, library and school there is an altar dedicated to the appropriate muse. You can see these spirits benevolently partnering and inspiring the activities.

In the hills behind the city are several temples, one dedicated to the angel of the city herself, another to the angel of the mountains and yet another to the spirits of fertility that watch over the land.

You are free to wander through this city on your own. Stay relaxed and enjoy your impressions. Take as long as you want.

Give yourself at least five minutes to contemplate and move around the city. You need to be in a day-dreamy mood, without falling asleep or your mind wandering off.

When you are ready, bring yourself back to the harbour. Before re-embarking on your boat, perhaps you would like to light a flame or give an offering of thanks. Get in the boat. The ocean current carries you away, sprites and mermaids gracefully dancing around your journey.

When you are ready, bring your awareness fully into your body and the room where you are. Touch yourself. Stretch. You may want to make some notes or do a drawing of your experience.

The city of angels exists in different forms in every human community. In the modern world, particularly with the noise, human throng and traffic fumes, it is difficult to imagine and sense these realities, but they are there. Wherever there is human culture you will find angels and spirits interwoven with it. Whether it is an Amazonian tribal village or ancient Athens or modern Delhi or Buenos Aires, the spirits are there.

All these angels hold in their energy fields blueprints of the highest human ideals. People who come within the angels' aura are unconsciously affected by them and inspired. So the statues of justice that stand over many law courts should not be dismissed as only symbolic, for they represent great angels who hold in their auras ideas of justice, deliberation, equality before the law and so on. Anyone who comes into court will find themselves being influenced and touched by these ideas. Think also of the altar to Mercury, god-angel of communication, which was tended at the main market in ancient Rome. Even now, for instance, a statue of the goddess Ceres – angel of grain and abundance – presides over the commodity market in Chicago. These are just a few among perhaps millions of examples.

Explore these realities for yourself. You can do the following exercise anywhere, but it is easiest near the place that you are studying.

EXPLORING ANGELS OF THE CITY

Go quiet in the way that best suits you.

When you feel calm and ready, begin to open your awareness to the particular place that interests you – a hospital, school, theatre, law court or seat of government – and become aware of its shape, purpose and contours.

Then begin to contemplate that there is an angel of this place. It overlights and permeates the place. It holds the highest ideals of how that place can function and fulfil its purpose.

Greet it. Fully acknowledge its presence. Notice your impressions.

In your contemplation explore how big this angel feels. Notice how many lesser spirits of the same kind are within its aura. Contemplate how it influences human behaviour.

To make a deeper connection with this angel you can of course make an offering to it.

From a centred attitude, contemplate what kind of offering might be appropriate. Perhaps you can light a candle at home. Perhaps you can take some grain or fruit to the place. Perhaps you need to go there and meditate or pray. There may be other actions you can take, such as joining or starting a local support group.

Give thanks for its presence and withdraw from the exercise.

As always, it is important to keep your imagination open. When some friends' children, for example, were about to start at secondary school, they realised that they could not clearly feel an angel of education overlighting the place. They went into meditation and attunement, and realised that they needed to strengthen the connection.

In the summer holidays my friends went to the school when there was no one around, taking with them a bag filled with hundreds of inexpensive gems and crystals. With the help of their children they planted the stones in the sports fields and gardens around the school.

It was, they said, one of those peculiar situations. They were mature adults apparently behaving like the most extreme kind of crystal flake, seeking to improve the quality of schooling for their children. They were relieved that no one saw them. And the children did fine.

THE FORM OF TOWNS AND CITIES

Even if people do not consciously recognise that their town or city has its angel, they may be unconsciously influenced. It is always interesting to observe the work of architects and town and city planners. The great challenge is to merge visual beauty with social needs. In fact, there are archetypal patterns of holy cities which work towards creating the ideal harmony.

The most famous of these patterns is that of a circular city with four gateways to the north, south, west and east. Four roads then come into the centre where there is a spring, fountain or body of water. This pattern is described in the New Testament's Book of Revelation, and some of the most beautiful Islamic palaces, such as the Alhambra in Grenada, Spain, are laid out on this plan.

The following exercise is best done with a group of friends so that you can compare notes afterwards. For people who are involved in community work and city planning, the exercise brings new and very supportive dimensions. It can carry on for several weeks, perhaps even longer.

Before you start doing the exercise, spend a while looking at maps of the city. Get a sense of its layout and different communities. Notice where the rivers and canals are. Notice the green areas. Be very aware of its hills and valleys. If you can, get hold of old maps to see what the city was like before all the building took place. Also look at a geological map to see what kind of foundations the city sits upon. Most of this information should be available in local libraries.

If you can, do the exercise on one of the city's sacred sites such as its cathedral or principal temple, or on a prominent hill where there was once a shrine, or by its river. If it is not possible to get to one of these places, do it at home or wherever you can find some calm.

TO CONNECT WITH THE ANGEL OF YOUR CITY
OR TOWN

In the way that works best for you, go silent and come to centre.

When you are ready, begin to extend your awareness out across the city. Be aware of the shape and contours of the land. Spend a while looking carefully at its landscape.

Then, when you are ready, take your awareness towards the centre of the city. Contemplate the possibility of a wonderful angelic being whose aura extends to envelop the whole city. This angel is capable of understanding all the needs and dynamics of its community.

Stay quiet for a while, open to the possibility of its existence. Notice any impressions.

Then deliberately, aloud or telepathically, communicate that you would like to connect more consciously with it. Ask to make the connection. Watch your impressions.

In particular notice whether it feels appropriate to make a gesture or offering to the angel – then or later. Notice whether you feel that you should visit any particular spots in the city and make offerings or prayers. Be open to any suggestion.

When you feel that you have some connection, allow your awareness to blend with the angel's. This means a deeper relaxation and opening to its energy.

Then allow your consciousness to feel and sense the city as if you were the angel itself. Allow your awareness to flow down and through the city with it. Notice your impressions. In particular, take your awareness into the parks, hospitals, theatres, museums, schools and so on. Also take your awareness into the areas where there is poverty and violence. Get a sense of the whole community from the angel's perspective.

When you feel that you have had enough, bring your awareness back to cover the whole city. Then gently bring your focus back down into your own body.

Give thanks.

During this exercise you may receive an impression or

suggestion for some action. Look at the suggestion carefully and, if it harms no one, do it.

Angels of Nations and Folk Spirits

Nations as a whole have angels which encompass in their consciousness the history, ecology and cultures of their peoples. In political terms, these spirits are particularly interesting. History has often imposed territorial boundaries that are not harmonious with the folk spirits. Looking at a map, almost every time that you see a straight line you can be certain that military or political force has imposed a rigid division without any awareness of or care for the local ecology and culture.

A senior executive in the United Nations went on many foreign trips from his base in Geneva. On these trips, over weekends when he was not working, he would often lead workshops in which a group would explore their *Volkgeist* or folk spirit. He said that the most interesting session he ever led was in South Africa in the 1970s. As people were led through the meditations, they encountered a number of different spirits all seeking to accommodate each other. There was the angel of the Zulu nation, as well as angels of other southern African tribes. There was also the folk spirit of the Boers, which was in itself related to the folk spirit of Holland. And, of course, there was the *Volkgeist* of the British.

All these angels were seeking to come into harmony. In the group sessions, black South Africans were, to their surprise, moved and touched by the Boer spirit. The white people were also equally moved by their connection with the angel of the Zulus.

In the eighteenth and nineteenth centuries there was much discussion about these spirits. The great German philosopher Hegel suggested that the supreme achievement for humanity was to facilitate the full incarnation of these spirits into their nation states. Some of these ideas, as stated earlier, were adopted and perverted by Hitler's National Socialists. Their interpretation of this concept was in direct opposition to the original perception of folk spirits which, in the words of another famous German philosopher, Herder, were all varied flowers in the same garden – each to be respected and nurtured.

Before doing the following exercise to connect with folk spirits it may be worthwhile to look at the symbols and distinctive features of the nation with which you are working. There is always a flag and some kind of anthem, and usually animals or plants or particular places that are considered important to its history. Look also for folk heroes and the myths and legends that belong exclusively to that nation.

This can be a very powerful and moving experience because you are connecting with some of the great forces, hopes and tragedies of history – resonances of which are all held in the Angel's aura. If at any point you begin to feel overwhelmed, gently withdraw your attention, turn your focus down and into your own body, and end the exercise.

CONNECTING WITH THE FOLK SPIRIT

In the way that best suits you, go quiet and come to centre.

Let your awareness begin to travel out across the landscape of the country. Be aware of its size and of the contours, hills and mountains, rivers and lakes.

Be aware of its natural borders and also of its political borders – these are often different. Notice them and move on. Be aware of the sea or ocean that may be around the country. Let any other natural features come into your awareness.

When you are ready, begin to lift your awareness above the land and gently upwards. Over the land, huge and aware, is a presence that fully knows and loves the landscape that it overlights. Spend a while opening up and sensing this great spirit. Notice any impressions.

This may be enough for the first session. But if you feel ready, continue with the next part.

Very carefully and slowly, begin to take your attention down into the world of human ideas. Remember that people's thoughts and ideas are energy clouds that float around.

There is a realm here where three dynamics meet:

- The energy and flow of the landscape.
- The thoughts and ideas of the people.
- The vision, love and blueprint of the folk spirit, the overlighting angel.

This is a very interesting and complex energy field to contemplate. Stay relaxed and present to it. Notice your impressions and sensations. Notice how the three meet.

When you are ready, withdraw your attention and end the exercise.

At the end of both the exercises above, you can of course deepen your connection with the angel.

Telepathically reach out to the angel and gratefully acknowledge its presence.

There are two things you can ask to help your relationship with it.

- Is there anything I can do to acknowledge you that would be meaningful and authentic?
- To help bring your vision for the nation to fulfilment, are there any actions that I can take?

After asking both questions, just be patient and contemplative. Notice what passes through your mind. Assess the wisdom of your impressions. If, after reflection, it seems appropriate, act upon them.

Angels of Ceremony

The evolution of certain specialist spirits has led them to work in particular fields such as the arts or healing or some other part of human culture. Taking religious ordination as an example, behind all the formal ceremony of enrolment and dedication the candidate is also receiving a spirit which belongs to that particular religious form. Through the harmonic resonance of that deva, the person ordained is now permanently connected to the energy field and the ideas which belong to his religious group. Furthermore, if he or she uses certain symbolic words or gestures, the spirit opens up the flows of religious and healing energy associated with that religion.

You can see this in the Christian mass or communion. The priest goes through a very distinct set of words and gestures. The deva sets up the harmonics of connection and a real sense of sacramental blessing ensues. The same happens in many other religions. The most bizarre aspect is that the priest may be psychologically and physically degenerate, yet the blessing still comes through. In fact, it is almost a caricature that a priest can be drunk and careless but the ceremony works.

From a mystic point of view, this is the real source of the great argument between the Catholic and Orthodox Christian Churches on one side and the Protestant Churches on the other. The Catholics claim that Protestant priests do not go through the right ceremonies of ordination and, from our perspective, therefore do not have their devas of ordination. Because of this, they cannot properly perform the Church's ceremonies and bring through the appropriate energy and blessing. They simply do not have the angelic connection.

This angelic connection made at ordination can be seen at work in very powerful ways by religious leaders who carry what is called 'lineage'. These are men and women who have been ritually inducted into caring for and leading their religious group. When they are given their office they are also given the permanent angels which connect them to their group's energy field.

This can be extremely powerful. When, for example, people come into the presence of the Dalai Lama they are often stunned by the energy field around him. When someone who carries a lineage gives a blessing, the energy that comes through them is not coming simply from their own personal access to spirit but also from all the fields connected with their angels. Again, this can lead to paradoxical situations in which corrupt religious leaders are nevertheless able to generate beautiful atmospheres and give useful blessings.

Animal Totems

Finally, there are guardian spirits of animals who work with people. Tribal peoples have often felt that particular animals provide a model of behaviour that is appropriate for them to copy. A male bear, for example, is a strong and self-reliant creature who knows how to eat well in the summer and hibernate in the winter. An elephant, on the other hand, though also strong, is sensitive and loyal to its family group. Animals also have distinct relationships with their habitats and, when these environments change, they adapt their behaviour.

Earlier it was explained that species of animals, like species of plants, have their own angels which carry the blueprints for that type of animal. Many tribal societies felt a mystical connection with certain animals and made clear and specific relationships with their angels.

To gain wisdom and support from these animals, the priests of the tribe might, for example, wear robes made from the animal's skin and perform dances that imitated its movements. This would be their method for attuning to the totem and coming into telepathic resonance with it.

In Peru, for example, the Matses hold the jaguar spirit sacred as their totem. Nearly all adults are tattooed around their mouths to give them the appearance of the jaguar's wide 'smile'. Splinters from palm trees, representing whiskers, protrude from the lips of the men and through the noses of the women. In the Sudan, the Nuer priests always wear leopard skins when performing ceremonies in order to channel the power of the leopard spirit.

When I lived in Morocco I spent some time in a village whose spirit was the goat. Several times a year they performed a musical ceremony in which one of the village boys dressed as a goat and danced as the goat spirit. The boy usually took this role for a number of years. Men who had been the goat as boys were often considered to have magical powers, especially in the field of fertility. One of these men who I knew carried a powerful, sensuous and musky atmosphere. When he had a sexual relationship with a woman whom Western medicine had condemned as totally infertile, she quickly became pregnant.

All this is relevant to individuals as well as to groups. Contemporary students of shamanism and tribal religions have found it useful to discover which animal spirits relate to their spiritual growth and personal transformation.

There are various ways of identifying your animal totem. All basically consist of taking you into a deeply relaxed state and then allowing your subconscious awareness to scan the different animal spirits until one of them comes into a harmonic relationship with you. This animal spirit will be the one which best matches your personality and soul patterns.

FINDING YOUR ANIMAL SPIRIT

This exercise can take twenty minutes so make sure that you are comfortable. In your own way, go silent and very relaxed.

When you are ready, begin to imagine that you have chosen to go swimming in the most friendly lake or pool in the world. You are in the water and the temperature is absolutely perfect for you. You feel good and strong. Without any trouble, you are able to swim and move like a fish. Being under the water is easy and wonderful.

When you are ready, swim slowly down to the bottom of the lake and there you will discover a tunnel. In perfect safety enter and swim down and along this long tunnel.

After a while the tunnel opens up into a warm and beautiful cave. Come out of the water and look around this friendly space within the earth.

At the end of the cave is an entrance to another, smaller tunnel. Move towards this entrance and go through it. You now find yourself on a long set of steps which go down and down into the earth. Go down these steps. It feels warm and interesting.

Then you begin to notice and sense some light and fresh air at the end of the tunnel.

You come out of the tunnel and find yourself on the edge of the most wonderful and friendly jungle. The sky is blue and the sun mellow and affectionate.

When you are ready, go into the jungle.

Now that you are in the jungle, wait patiently. One of the animals in this place will come and present itself to you three times, each time from a different angle. This is your totem. Wait patiently and let it come.

Do not accept an animal that bares its teeth at you or has an aggressive attitude towards you. Be open to impressions. Sometimes people receive more than one animal.

If you have no success in the jungle, there is another place you can go.

Stay relaxed. Go back to the entrance to the steps which brought you down to the jungle. Go through the entrance and you will find another tunnel that you had not noticed before. Go into this tunnel.

This tunnel opens into a great cave which is filled with good friends and ancestors. Relax with them.

At one end of the cave a fire is burning, throwing up shadows and smoke. You become fascinated by the shadows and smoke. You relax again and allow yourself to be mesmerised by the shadows and smoke.

Out of this mist an animal appears to you. It appears to you again and then again.

When you have met your spirit animal, stay with it for a while. See if it has anything to communicate to you or to show you. Perhaps it has a gift for you.

Give thanks and tell the animal that you will never forget it. Ask for a deepening of the relationship.

When you are ready, begin to withdraw your attention.

Go back up the steps until you come to the small cave. Enter the warm water and swim back up to the beautiful lake. Come out of the lake.

In real life now, stretch and touch your body. You may feel like having a little shake. Look around the space where you are. Touch yourself. Be fully present.

When you have discovered your totem you can research your animal through books and pictures. Watch some wildlife documentaries and learn its behaviour patterns, which can help you in your daily life. Also, when you are in psychological distress you can go quiet within yourself and contemplate your animal spirit. Many people find this protective and comforting.

10

Into the Future

WHENEVER I AM contacted by newspaper or television researchers looking for a story on angels, I am always very careful. Are they looking to make fun of it? Are they seeking sensationalism? Are they serious?

Nobody is being burnt any more for these beliefs. The Churches have lost their power to persecute. Nevertheless an aura of disbelief remains. But it is dispersing.

It is dispersing partly because people in general need a new freedom of expression and experience. And we now have simply too much information, too many experiences, too much important cultural history to deny the possibility of the spirit world. The essential dynamic of life on our planet demands that we come back to truth and a realisation of our true environment.

Disdain for the spirit world is a disdain for the sacred beauty inherent in every aspect of life. It leads to a crass and destructive materialism, the results of which are only too obvious. A recovery of our relationship with the world of spirits is a step forward in our spiritual freedom. Animism was once a natural, powerful force for good. It was a part of normal, everyday life. It can be normal again.

Scientific Justification

One way of being thought 'normal' in today's society is to be able to justify metaphysical phenomena with scientific theories. In the nineteenth century, for instance, psychics and telepaths enjoyed the invention of the telephone and wireless. Here was technology which could be used to explain the invisible phenomena of psychism and telepathy.

More recently, the language of sub-atomic physics has been used to justify and explain classic mystical ideas. Even if the theories do not exactly match the mystic dynamics, at the very least they provide a 'scientific' and respectable language for discussion. People working in holistic medicine and therapy are also always looking for new medical research to justify what they are doing.

In fact, scientific research and theories are bit by bit creaking their way towards realities and information which mystics and energy-workers have known and understood for ages. It is wonderful to watch it catching up with reality. The Newtonian worldview completely ditched any scientific understanding that was not completely logical and testable, but it is finally coming of age. In particular, the realities of quantum mechanics and the theories of chaos, catastrophe and emergence are once again allowing us the freedom to think and talk intelligently about inner dynamics that are not necessarily logical or testable by mechanical means.

Chaos Theory and Coherence

Where do angels fit into this? At the moment I see three converging theories which are very interesting. The first is chaos and emergence theory.

One of the greatest and most important insights of chaos theory is that when you get enough random particles, they will suddenly organise themselves. There is some design factor built into the universe that, despite chaotic beginnings and unrelated factors, draws things into coherent form – stars into galaxies, traders and buyers into economies, cells into trees, minuscule movements into general waves. Anyone who has looked at the beauty of a computer-generated fractal design will know that a simple pattern randomly repeated emerges into a general form that has beauty and integrity. Things do not remain chaotic. They emerge into coherent form.

Working in a presently unknown dimension is some kind of magnetic or attractive agent which draws all emerging properties into coherence. In scientific theory these agents are called attractors. There is some kind of magnetic flow in the universe that draws everything into certain rhythms, changes and fulfilments.

It is clear that there is some kind of relationship between these attractors and angelic realities. It may be that devas in general are these attractors – the mediators who hold the specific blueprints for all the different things that exist in this kaleidoscopic universe.

Morphic Resonance

There is also the new theory of morphic resonance and morphogenetic fields. Initiated by the school of organismic philosophy, it has been more recently developed and brought to public attention by the biologist-philosopher Rupert Sheldrake. This theory suggests that all organisms have an invisible energy field around them which carries that organism's history and which communicates to other morphic fields of the same type of organism.

This is very close to the inner reality. Many people feel that this theory is important because it helps to reclaim an understanding of life that is respectful of other dimensions. It questions a mechanical understanding of evolution, which is almost completely driven by chance and environmental circumstances, and replaces it with something more creative, eccentric and purposeful.

From the perspective of this book, however, there is one more step to take in this theory. This is to appreciate that these morphic fields are alive and conscious in their own right. They are in fact the devas, angels and spirits.

Holograms

The third set of theories is associated with holograms and David Bohm's idea of an implicate order to life. What Bohm suggests and what holograms actually demonstrate is that everything is enfolded upon itself. If you take a hologram and break it up, every single bit of it still holds the whole picture. Bohm suggested, from a philosophical and mathematical perspective, that within everything is everything else.

From an angelic perspective this is certainly true. Because of their harmonic resonance with each other and the universe, they have no experience of separation even if they perform different roles. The lesser deva is always within the blueprint of the greater deva, who is in turn a lesser deva to a larger and more inclusive spirit.

Also, as suggested earlier in this book, an understanding of devas goes some way to solving one of the great challenges in modern science – which asks how everything is held together. What is the glue, the magnetism, that holds together atoms, molecules, suns and galaxies? Mainstream science has a major expansion to make in its understanding of the world. It will find its unified theory in a parallel world of devas which is interconnected with the material world.

All of these theories can only be fully understood in the context of understanding that angels are not simply glorious golden beings, but an essential part of the universal fabric.

Social Justification

There is also huge social and environmental justification for this rebirth of angelic awareness. When people really want and need something, historic miracles happen. Dividing walls and totalitarian regimes collapse. Political prisoners are released from prison and become president of their nation. The extremes of contemporary medicine begin to give way to a wiser and more holistic approach. Crude, impersonal forms of psychology start to be replaced by a more humane understanding.

Respect for the beauty and life in everything is also coming. After almost fifteen hundred years we are finally moving away from a culture of superstition and spiritual manipulation. We live in a new age of free-flowing information. Telephones, desktop publishing, free media and the Internet mean that open debate and challenges to unnecessary authority and bigotry are now ingrained in our culture. In this open arena of free information, superstition and flakiness will be challenged; at the same time, the oppressive culture that scorns spirits will itself be scorned.

The natural acceptance of the spirit world will enhance society and culture, and support creative ways of handling contemporary social and ecological problems. The basis of this support will be the sacred respect and wise attunement given to all human and natural communities. The landscape, plant life and all living creatures will be honoured. The cities and towns will be communities of nurture and creativity.

In the anthology *Devas and Men* A.E. Wodehouse compares the relationship between people and devas to the warp and woof in weaving. One set of threads runs up and down while the other set is woven in from side to side – no cloth is possible without them interweaving.

> The business of human creation is not to smother and conceal the devic warp. Rather the health and life of all human arts and institutions, all religions and civilisations will depend almost entirely on how far the underlying warp is permitted to show through. For if the devic threads are overlaid too heavily, and if the glowing life and colour in them is thereby stifled and concealed, such a thickening of the human woof is always disastrous. It is the unfailing mark of the decay of the art, the decline of the civilisation, the corruption and devitalising of the religion.

Psychological Support

The psychological support for a rebirth of animism is also immense. In a sense the whole of this book, in particular the chapters on healing and on the angels that help humanity, is about this psychological dimension.

Like every other aspect of life, we are destined to fulfil ourselves and achieve our true potential. This is no different from a flower or a star system. But human beings are complex and sensitive creatures. We have trouble lifting our awareness out of the overload and stimulation of everyday life. We find it difficult to handle our challenges, frustrations and sicknesses. Our emotions and minds are easily overwhelmed. We therefore often harden ourselves in order to survive. It seems we have little choice – crumble into burn-out, or put on our shields and survive.

An understanding of the inner dimensions, the opening of relationships with the spirits, provides a new dimension to our lives. We begin to sense new colours and sounds and feelings. A new beauty and a new creativity enter our lives.

In his poem 'Pauline' Robert Browning wrote about the angelic muses that fed his creativity.

> *And of my powers, one springs up to save*
> *From utter death a soul with such desire*
> *Confined to clay – of powers the only one*
> *That marks me – an imagination which*
> *Has been a very angel, coming not*
> *In fitful visions, but beside me ever*
> *And never failing me.*

The angels bring useful qualities, and without the usual human baggage. There are no judgements, no fear, no need for gratification. Humans need comfort, success, love *now*. Waiting is painful. Devas, open to the complete cycle of everything, have no sense of the friction of time. Yet they exist fully within and alongside us. R.J. Stewart wrote a lovely verse which he entitled 'The Faery Folk':

> *If my humanity I'd loose,*
> *Which seduction would I choose?*
> *The angels' voice eternal in the stars,*
> *Or faery folk, immortal mid the flowers?*
>
> *The angels sing of boundless light and joy*
> *And spirit's flight to high rebirth,*
> *The faery folk are in the land*
> *And love the sacred earth.*

Choosing to Be Aware

I want people to see and feel the beauty and wonder of life. If someone has that sense of respect and wonder, who cares if they believe in angels?

The real challenge is to find a way of being entranced by angelic reality and, at the same time, fully engaged in daily life.

A division between the two kinds of awareness seems natural, but it is not: it is created by the culture in which we are brought up. Don't think of angels while you are driving, or you will crash your car! Don't be attuned to deva realities whilst running your business, or you will be seen as naive and go bankrupt! But this is all nonsense. Attunement to the spirit world means being in the real three-dimensional solid world and at the same time always knowing and feeling the other underlying dimensions.

But to turn our attention to the deva reality means that we have to change gear, to take ourselves into a different vibration and mood. This is not easy. Once we are in a groove we become addicted to it. Moving from the harsh and speedy vibrations of modern life to a more graceful mood is as difficult as giving up any other addiction like nicotine or alcohol or sugar.

Much of the hostility to angels and to people interested in them comes from those who unconsciously know how painful it would be for them to change mood and appreciate the deva magic. Sometimes you can almost feel their body and brain screaming that they could never make that change. But of course they could.

The mood that has us accustomed to the harshness of daily life can often be easily tamed and led into another more gentle groove. There are horses for courses and different people have their own methods: music, sport, walking, cooking, landscape, making love, dancing, caring ... in these activities people move into different moods. The great challenge is to stay in that mood when you go back to everyday realities and overload. How can you do this?

It needs a clear, conscious and purposeful decision to stay aware and connected to the spirit dimension, to see the beauty and magic. It needs a decision to be aware of all the realities, not just the one social dimension. The underlying realities do not disappear because you are not aware of them. They are always there. Your body is still made of elementals even when you are driving your car, washing up or in the office. The landscape is teeming with invisible life, dancing and sparkling in the universal context. The city spirits are harmonically holding their visions of perfection. The muses are inspiring. The healing angels are overlighting and guiding. This is all there, no matter where your consciousness is focussed.

It is simply a matter of choosing to remember, choosing to be aware. Do you want to remember this reality? Ask this question of yourself right now. If the answer is yes, pledge yourself this second to remember. Stretch your awareness out to all the angel realms, from single atom to cosmos, and affirm that you will remember, you will stay aware, you will stay cooperative.

What help do you need? It is so easy for us to forget and slip back into the sleep of non-awareness. Perhaps you need a daily ritual to start the day, such as lighting a candle or making offerings to the spirit of your house or town. Perhaps your kitchen or office or car needs some image or sculpture or object to remind and help you.

This, then, is the last exercise.

COMMITMENT AND HELP

Go silent in your own way, and in the silence contemplate how meaningful and beautiful and creative this inner world is.

Then, when you are ready, look to see what action will support you in maintaining this remembrance and awareness.

You can ask your guardian angel for help. You can ask all the spirits for help. And you will receive it.

Give thanks.

Resources

Selected Further Reading

ALTMAN, Nathaniel, *The Deva Handbook*, Destiny Books, 1995

ANDREWS, Ted, *Animal-Speak*, Llewellyn, 1995

BAILEY, Alice, *A Treatise on Cosmic Fire*, Lucis Press, 1970

BLOOM, William, *The Sacred Magician*, Gothic Image, 1992

BLOOM, William, *Psychic Protection*, Piatkus, 1996

BRIGGS, Katherine, *An Encyclopaedia of Fairies*, Pantheon Books, 1976

CAMPBELL, Joseph, *Primitive Mythology*, Penguin, 1987

CHALLONER, H.K., *Watchers of the Seven Spheres*, Routledge, 1933

CHALLONER, H.K., *Devas and Men: A Compilation of Theosophical Studies on the Angelic Kingdom*, Quest, 1977

BOHM, David, *Wholeness and the Implicate Order*, Routledge and Kegan Paul, 1980

BROOKE, Elizabeth, *Women Healers Throughout History*, The Women's Press, 1993

FINDHORN COMMUNITY, *The Findhorn Garden*, Harper & Row, 1975

FOX, Matthew, and Rupert Sheldrake, *The Physics of Angels*,

HarperCollins, 1996

FRAZER, James, *The Golden Bough*, Macmillan, many editions

HUMANN, Harvey, *The Many Faces of Angels*, DeVorss, 1988

HODSON, Geoffrey, *The Coming of the Angels*, Rider, 1932

HODSON, Geoffrey, *Brotherhood of Angels and Men*, Theosophical Society, 1941

HODSON, Geoffrey, *The Kingdom of the Gods*, Theosophical Society, 1952

INGERMAN, Sandra, *Soul Retrieval*, HarperCollins, 1991

KEIGHTLEY, Thomas, *The World Guide to Gnomes, Fairies, Elves and Other Little People*, Avenel Books, 1978

MACLEAN, Dorothy, *To Hear the Angels Sing*, Turnstone Press, 1980

MACLEAN, Dorothy, *Choices of Love*, Lindisfarne, 1998

LEADBEATER, C.W. *The Science of the Sacraments*, Theosophical Publishing House, 1932

PARISEN, Maria, (ed), *Angels and Mortals – Their Creative Power*, Quest, 1990

POGACNIK, Marko, *Nature Spirits and Elemental Beings – Working with the Intelligence in Nature*, Findhorn Press, 1997

SAUNDERS, Nicholas, *Animal Spirits*, Macmillan, 1995

SCOTT, Cyril, *Music: Its Secret Influence*, Routledge, 1934

SHELDRAKE, Rupert, *A New Science of Life*, Blond & Briggs, 1981

SMALL WRIGHT, Machaelle, *Behaving as if the God in All Life Mattered: A New Age Ecology*, Perelandra, 1987

SPENCE, Lewis, *British Fairy Origins*, Aquarian Press, 1981

STEWART, R.J., *The Living World of Faery*, Gothic Image, 1995

Tapes, Workshops and Mailings

If you would like to know more about William Bloom's tapes and workshops, or be put on his mailing list, please contact:

Holistic Partnerships
10 The Murreys
Ashtead
Surrey
KT21 2LU
Tel/Fax: 01372 272 400
email: welcome@holisticpartnerships.com
Or visit his website at www.williambloom.com

Index

Index

earth 10, 43–4, 47, 58, 76, 78, 103–5
earthquakes 44
earthworms 44
education, spirit of 51, 142–3
Egyptian civilization 52
elementals 10, 41, 44–6, 47, 54–5, 57–8, 59, 103–5, 108
   body 117–20, 124
   pathological 124–6
elves 3, 37–9, 57–8, 72, 106–7, 130
emotional and mental energy 50, 59, 93–5
energy fields 32, 41–2, 65–6, 75–8, 155
England 39, 51–2
environment
   human relationship with 14–15
   see also landscape spirits
eroticism 5
esoteric mysticism 11
etheric energy 76
Eucharist 34, 148
Euphrates river 45
evolution of devas 57–9

fairies 10, 11, 43, 53–4, 58, 61–2, 72, 79, 80, 106–7
fairy rings 37–9
fauns 42, 43, 48, 57
Findhorn Foundation 108
fire 10, 43, 46, 59, 103–5
folklore 4
   religious 3
folk spirit *see Volkgeist*
form, creation of 54–5
fountains 9
Frazer, Sir James 48
freedom of expression 60–1
freemasonry 34, 53
Freud, Sigmund 25, 34

Ganges river 45
gardening 16–17, 22, 30–1, 79, 80, 91–2, 108–10
gases 59
George, Saint 51–2
gestures, symbolic 97, 98, 99, 148
gifts 10
Glastonbury 44, 49, 106
gnomes 10, 44, 57–8, 76, 108
Gnosis 11, 52
goblins 44, 47
gods and goddesses 10, 11
Grateful Dead 89
Greek civilization 5, 11, 68
green men 48
Grimms' Fairy Tales 6
group karma 113–14
guardian angels 26–7, 34–5, 80, 133–7, 139–47

Harare 49
Hartley, Christine 33
healing 10, 16–17, 30–1, 79, 80, 111–32
   healing spirits 45, 51, 79, 80, 114–32

landscape 110
   self-healing 128
Hegel, Georg Wilhelm Friedrich 145
Herder, Johann Gottfried 146
Hinduism 46, 52
hobgoblins 44
Hodson, Geoffrey 126
holistic medicine 65, 114, 117, 154
holograms 155–6
homeopathy 120–1
household objects 10
household spirits 2–3, 10, 20, 24, 30, 74, 82–4, 160
Hsun Tzu 21
human beings
   emotional and mental energy 50, 59, 93–5
   human-angel relationship 95–6
   souls 111–13, 134, 136–7
   spirits related to 50–2
human spirits 133

illness and disease 112–32
images, sensing spirits by 41–3, 51, 64–5, 67, 70–1
inspiration 19–24, 100–2
inviting spirits to connect 23–4, 31, 97–100
Ireland 4
Islam 12, 14, 52

Jerusalem 49
Judaism 11, 14
Jung, Carl 12
justice, spirit of 51, 141

Kailas, Mount 49, 105
Kensington Gardens 33
Knights Templar 52–3
Krishnamurti 34

lakes 10, 44, 49
landscape spirits 37–9, 45, 49, 74, 101, 105–6, 107–10
Leadbeater, C.W. 12, 47
ley lines 44
lineage 148
little people 4
living patterns *see* blueprints
London 45, 71–2
   Angel of 35–7, 139

Maclean, Dorothy 54–5
magic 52–3
memories *see* blueprints
Mercury 11, 79, 80, 141
mermaids 45, 133
Milligan, Spike 33
morphogenetic fields 10, 155
mountains 10, 49, 105–6
muses 3, 10, 11, 51, 61, 76, 79, 86–90, 101–2
music 55–6, 89–90
mysticism 11, 52, 62–3, 136
mystic marriage 136